BOOMSTART

SuperLaws of Successful Entrepreneurs

Gary Rhoads
Michael Swenson
David Whitlark

Brigham Young University

Kendall Hunt
publishing company

Cover design created by Arturo Soza.

Kendall Hunt
p u b l i s h i n g   c o m p a n y

www.kendallhunt.com
Send all inquiries to:
4050 Westmark Drive
Dubuque, IA 52004-1840

Copyright © 2009 by Kendall Hunt Publishing Company

ISBN 978-0-7575-6623-3

Printed in the United States of America
10 9 8 7 6 5 4 3 2

*This book is dedicated to our families
who have encouraged us and given
so generously of their time and support
and to all intrepid entrepreneurs
who have shared their dreams,
setbacks, and victories—giving us
a privileged look into the magic
of entrepreneurial marketing.*

Contents

Successful startups have the Right Stuff. That is, they have an experienced and tenacious management team, a business model that generates revenue and profit, and an ability to tap into a deep understanding of customer needs and marketplace opportunities.

Entrepreneurs are by nature optimistic and believe they have a unique idea that the world has never seen and everyone will want to buy. However, experience shows that uniqueness does not come easily and must be earned by sharpening the angle.

Best Practices: Find Unsolved Pain, Make the Pitch, Dominate the Situation, Earn Credibility and Don't Buy It, Hit the Sweet Spot

To get your startup off the ground and increase your speed to market, you need a champion. Pick the best horses you can find and ride them all the way to the bank. After all, no entrepreneur is an island!

Best Practices: Find Benefactors, Prospect for Beta Goldmines, Survive on Rabbits . . . Feast on Elephants, Weigh Anchor, Make Heroes, Unleash the Love Group, Build Positive Mojo

Surround yourself with reputable people, ideas, and companies. Find ways to look big and play big, even if you're not big.

Best Practices: Feed a Frenzy, Be an Underdog, Hatch a Catchphrase, Reach out with Touch Points, Build a Spider Web

Great entrepreneurs are great inventors, but not necessarily great at inventing new technologies. They are great at inventing and doing marketing events. Put your creative thinking cap on! Get experiential! Create memorable experiences that people can take home with them!

Best Practices: Get Experiential, Have a Love Fest, Make Demonstrations Compelling

Perfect products don't guarantee entrepreneurial success. Combining a good product with a sharp angle directed at a high-value opportunity is more important than finding absolute perfection out of the starting gate. So don't wait for the perfect product; start reaping the rewards of your hard work as soon as possible. Most people are surprisingly forgiving when a fresh idea with real merit appears in the marketplace.

Best Practices: Be a Closer, Lower the Barriers, Price for Profit, Choose the Right Moment, Augment your Core

Applying the SuperLaws to a startup pays big dividends. Review some case studies to see how the audit identifies areas for improvement and how creative entrepreneurs use the results to drive their businesses to greater levels of success.

Introduction

Suppose you have an idea and are preparing to launch a new venture. How would you know if your idea is a good one? Moreover, how would you successfully launch your new product or service into our overcrowded, overhyped marketplace with little or no money? As entrepreneurship faculty, we have been asked these two questions over and over again. We used to give out top-of-mind textbook answers that sounded great, but lacked real-world relevance. But then we decided to make our answers smarter and began a quest to identify and learn the best practices and tactics of the successful entrepreneurs that we know and admire. After spending over 10 years observing and interviewing over 100 entrepreneurs, and starting five new ventures ourselves, we believe we have found a simple, yet powerful framework that provides the practical answers most needed to get new entrepreneurs up and running successfully.

Over the last few years, we have seen a tsunami of interest in launching new ventures. It seems like every day, our phone lines light up with aspiring entrepreneurs seeking feedback on their new megabuck ideas. We love the enthusiasm, but judging from what we have learned from successful entrepreneurs and venture capital firms, most new ideas for products or services are just "okay," and some are even really bad! To make matters worse, most people are blinded by their hopes for quick success and haven't learned to spot the differences between a good idea and a bad idea. They don't know what to change to make a good idea better. That's painful for them and us. On the other hand, from time to time we meet with entrepreneurs who have an uncanny ability or special knack of tweaking losers into winners.

This year, out of every 100 new ventures, only a few will succeed and many will fail. All that failure takes a heavy toll on individuals and our communities. As authors, we would like to see more new ventures succeed. **Boom Start** is about how *smart* entrepreneurs *quickly* go from good idea to great idea and to profitability. The book guides the reader through the mindset, tactics, and behaviors of successful entrepreneurs. We call it having the right stuff. We believe that **Boom Start** will change your perceptions about how top-gun entrepreneurs compete and succeed in today's markets. But, warning: as you read this book, you may have to put aside many traditional notions about marketing and business practices that emerge from corporate America. Big business strategies of the past simply don't work for shoestring-funded, tactic-focused entrepreneurs. Startups must play to their strengths and avoid emulating many time-honored practices of Fortune 500 companies who have millions to spend on product R&D and millions to spend on sophisticated messaging and promotional campaigns to buy market share. **Boom Start** entrepreneurs can't afford to buy success, so they must do it the old-fashioned way: they earn it through creative low-cost tactics.

The book highlights the five **SuperLaws** that we have uncovered in our study of entrepreneurs—Sharpen the Angle, Ride Horses, Play Big, Do an Event, Reap the Rewards—and their associated **Best Practices.** The SuperLaws and Best Practices can be used as a practical framework for determining the likelihood of product success. Each **SuperLaw** explains a basic principle in a logical and entertaining way; we show how startup companies succeed when they follow the laws and why they are more likely to fail when they violate the laws. The Best Practices offer tactical tips on how to quickly bring your new business in line with each SuperLaw.

If you are interested in starting a new company, start today by reading Chapter 1 to see if you have the right stuff. In Chapter 2, you learn how to take an *okay* or *good* product and **Sharpen the Angle** to become a product category dominator. Simply put, if your angle meets all five conditions of a powerful competitive angle, then you have a winner. If it doesn't, then it is probably stinko. But don't give up. Use the five components of an angle to modify or tweak your product until you get a winner. Chapter 3 teaches you to **Ride Horses** all the way to the bank. After all, experience and friendships count, but it doesn't have to be your own experience and friendships. You learn how to **Play Big** in Chapter 4, even though you're a small company. In Chapters 5 and 6, you'll gain insight into how to create memorable experiences with your customers by learning to **Do an Event**, and start **Reaping the Rewards** of your winning idea by accelerating the growth of your new venture. Finally, the book ends by demonstrating how to apply the SuperLaws start-to-finish to a business venture through doing a **Startup Audit**. Now we encourage you to read the book and wish you good fortune in starting your venture. Game on.

Right Stuff

Successful startups have the Right Stuff. That is, they have a pattern of doing the right things. They have an experienced and tenacious management team, a business model that generates revenue and profit, and an ability to tap into a deep understanding of customer needs and marketplace opportunities.

Every year we watch entrepreneurs pitch new business ideas. Every year we see one or two that we know will attract a lot of customer interest and investment dollars. They have that special something, almost a magical combination of drive, focus, and freshness of idea, that seems to guarantee success. We would like to see all startups be just as successful, but often it takes years and many missteps for entrepreneurs to find their way.

Recently we listened to a team pitching the idea of a Renaissance Fair complete with jousting knights, medieval village and villagers, stage performances, wandering minstrels, tart-selling wenches, newly planted forest, and a manmade lake. They were asking for millions of investment dollars. To show their idea had merit, they presented a marketing research study that concluded the majority of families in the area are in favor of more entertainment options, pointed out that the area is one of the few in the country without a Renaissance Fair, stated that the management team has many years of experience participating in such fairs, and bragged that their fair would be a model of environmental sustainability. Missing from the presentation, however, was any evidence that families in the area have any keen interest in Renaissance Fairs, hard numbers to show how many people will need to attend the fair each day for the enterprise to break even, ideas on how to attract new and repeat customers, or a plan to start small and expand as local interest grows.

Trumped-up marketing research studies, promises of limitless financial opportunity, and "out of the box" ideas don't impress venture capital firms, angel investors, or even those of us that know and teach entrepreneurship. Rather, we want answers to questions like "Why this?" "Why now?" "Why here?" and "Why you?" Don't be shocked or disheartened, but we have observed that professional investors have just as much interest in whether an entrepreneur can sell and manage an idea as in the idea itself.

While very few entrepreneurs need or qualify for the sort of funding that professional investors can offer, why wouldn't you want to put your new business on the same solid footing required by the big boys awarding venture capital? This book teaches entrepreneurs how to have the Right Stuff to succeed as a seat-of-the-pants, underfunded new business startup in a highly competitive international marketplace. Just because most entrepreneurs will never ask or get money from venture capital firms does not mean that they should not have as much chance for success as those that do!

Successfully Selling and Managing the Idea

Successful entrepreneurs often have great selling skills: that is a given. But for you to sell a new idea on a shoestring budget, customers really have to need what you are selling! Customers have to need it so bad that they are not only willing to pay the price to buy it, but also willing to help sell the product right along with you. But where do such ideas come from?

The evidence we've collected over the years suggests that entrepreneurs have a knack for finding good ideas and taking these good ideas and turning them into great ideas. No offense, but they are world-class snoops and we love them for it! They dig deep to unearth rough ideas and then refine them into silver and gold. We have a name for this talent: we call it R&D, which in entrepreneur-language stands for Rip Off and Design. They rip off ideas from their neighbors, but then redesign them into something much better—something that gets traction and generates attention.

And who are these good neighbors? Friends, family, relatives, employers, colleagues, connections, acquaintances, contacts, asso-

From Whence the Dream?

In recent years, entrepreneurs have come up with 71% of their ideas for new businesses by replicating or modifying an idea encountered through previous employment, 20% from serendipitous discovery, 5% by climbing on the computer technology bandwagon, and only 4% through systematic market research. Finding a good idea is easy. Finding and perfecting an angle is a challenge.

71%

20%

5%

4%

ciates, and businesses are all potentially "good neighbors." Everyone is the entrepreneur's neighbor. An *Inc. Magazine* study of the 500 fastest-growing companies shows that 71% of successful entrepreneurs replicate or modify an existing idea.[1] Another study shows that 43% of successful entrepreneurs get their winning ideas while working in the same industry or profession.[2]

With those sorts of numbers, the big temptation is simply to copy an existing idea with no change, no difference, no added value, and no new market. Seldom does this work, because customers do not feel compelled to buy a copycat product. There is no reason for customers to pay attention or make a change in their buying behavior. Entrepreneurial products must **stand for something different that is important**. The unique point of difference must be easily understood and highly valued by customers.

Once you've got that winning idea, successfully managing it often comes down to experience. Because there are so many things

---

[1] "How Entrepreneurs Craft Strategies that Work," by Amar Bhide, in *Harvard Business Review* (1994)

[2] "The Origins of Entrepreneurship," by John Case, in *Inc. Magazine* (June 1989)

to think about and so many things that can go wrong when starting a new business, there seems to be no substitute for having been there and done that. Often, the breadth of experience needed to establish a successful startup comes with a heavy financial and emotional price tag.

We have written this book to give readers a quick infusion of experience. We present the best and worst of what we have seen over the past 20 years, together with what we have the all-out audacity to call the SuperLaws of successful entrepreneurs. The SuperLaws help us, and more importantly, entrepreneurs, view their ideas and businesses through a new set of lenses. We are marketing professors and love basic concepts such as the 4Ps (product, place, price, promotion), STPs (segmentation, targeting, positioning), and USPs (unique selling propositions) as much as the next guy, but have found that entrepreneurs want and need much more than the basics.

The five SuperLaws are (1) sharpen the angle, (2) ride horses, (3) play big, (4) do an event, and (5) reap the rewards. Once an entrepreneur addresses the SuperLaws when charting out how to sell and manage their idea, it is easy to answer why this, why now, why here, and why you. But before we get started on the Super-Laws, let's turn for a moment to look at several examples of great startup ideas as well as introduce a few more basic ingredients of entrepreneurial "right stuff."

Pucker Up—Lip Balm on a Leash

When brothers Brady and Jeff Anderton, avid skiers, wakeboarders, mountain bikers, and hikers, discovered that their family, friends, and neighbors frequently lost containers of lip balm, they came up with a better idea. Why not put the lip balm on a leash? "Let's borrow the lip balm idea from neighbors—all lip balm manufacturers—and make it better." Leashes help us keep track of dogs and car keys. They may work for lip balm. Out of this thinking, Chap-Grip® Lip Balm and Leashables® were born. No more chapped and sore lips because you can't find your lip balm. With Chap-Grip you can clip it to almost anything—belt loop, key ring, jacket zipper. No more dry lips thanks to a better idea that is important to consumers—lip balm on a leash.

Superoots Air-Pot Gets to the Root of the Problem

Growing trees in containers is becoming quite common as more tree growers are converting from field growing to container growing every year. A major concern with this method of growing trees is the potential for root circling. The flat surfaces in traditional rigid containers and pots deflect tree roots, which can start the spiraling process. This is particularly troublesome for growers of "difficult" species, which simply do not do well in a rigid container, and for growers who suffer losses caused by heat in the summer or cold and wet in the winter. As the tree grows, these circling patterns may cause permanent damage to the root system, affecting the overall health of the tree. Trees with circling roots do not anchor well in the ground. Such trees may blow over or simply fall over. Trees with circling roots are not efficient at absorbing nutrients. Malnourished trees are highly susceptible to disease. Trees with circling roots may die as the spiraling roots eventually choke the tree.

This big problem for tree growers led to a big opportunity for ISA Certified Arborist and entrepreneur Ben Walker and his son Brandt of Canby, Oregon. Ben and Brandt discovered a unique growing container from a neighbor one-third of the way around the world—the Caledonian Tree Company of Edinburgh, Scotland. The unique container, called the Superoots Air-Pot, uses air to keep tree roots from circling as they mature. Tree roots grow toward holes in the sides of the pot. Once they reach the air hole, roots stop growing. This air-pruning technology eliminates circling roots as well as increases root development. The tree then sends out new roots. As this process continues, the tree develops a strong, straight root system. Benefits to the garden centers and nurseries include healthier trees and extended shelf life. For end-users, the fibrous, white-tipped roots perform better upon transplant.

Ben and Brandt purchased a license for a good idea—the Superoots Air-Pot—from a neighbor in Scotland and made it a great idea by creating SuperTrees brand trees. Combining the Air-Pot containers from Scotland with the productive tree-growing environment of the Willamette Valley in Oregon, Ben and Brandt are proving that better roots grow better trees. Today they supply SuperTrees brand trees to most of the western United States and they are growing! So, maybe money does grow on trees.

Climb to the Top with a Better Ladder— Little Giant Ladder Systems

How do you make a better ladder? Just ask Hal Wing. Over 30 years ago, he discovered a remarkable German inventor, Walter Kummerlin, who invented an all-in-one articulated ladder. At the time, Hal and Walter were neighbors in Germany. Hal immediately recognized that this innovative ladder could take the place of several ordinary ladders—a "Swiss Army Knife" of ladders. In 1972, he started importing these ladders from Germany. Notice that Hal took a good idea to a new market.

When Hal encountered problems with supply and exchange rate fluctuations, he quickly decided he could improve on his neighbor's good idea. He believed he could make it a great idea. While many experts characterized the ladder industry as a mature, high-volume, low-margin market, Hal considered the existing designs and asked, "How can we make this better, safer, and stronger?" He upgraded the original German ladder design and improved fabrication techniques. The result is the Little Giant, an adjustable ladder system that offers the versatility of 24 ladders in one. Even with price points three to four times higher than an ordinary A-frame ladder, the Little Giant sells millions because the adaptable design eliminates the need for multiple ladders and is so safe and reliable. Little Giant is selling more than a ladder: they are selling a lifetime of safety.

When the company hired Dean Johnson and Robin Hartl of the syndicated home-improvement show *Hometime* to host an infomercial, sales skyrocketed. The company managed to keep pace with demand by manufacturing 24/7. Revenues first sextupled and then increased another 40% in the following year. The company now grosses in nine figures. Today, Wing Enterprises holds worldwide patents and trademarks on many innovations in ladder design and manufacturing. The company is the largest manufacturer of American-made ladders. For Hal Wing, it's been a wonderful climb to the top because he turned a good idea into a great idea.

We admire entrepreneurs because they have a knack for adding value to everyday products or finding new ways to solve everyday problems. Great entrepreneurs are great observers of the everyday and are happy to leave blue-sky product development to others.

Knowing What's What over Gut

New businesses shouldn't fall victim to "paralysis by analysis," nor should they "fly by the seat of their pants." Balance "gut feel" with market and marketing research to put new businesses on the right track! Even entrepreneurs need to take time to test the power of their gut.

Occasionally we play a game with aspiring entrepreneurs who want to learn a few things about effective advertising and sales materials. First, we provide them with three time-tested rules of thumb for judging good print advertising from bad. Then we show them ad pairs. The ad pairs, provided by the research firm Roper Starch, show one ad that performs below norm for the product category and one ad that performs above norm based on their extensive library of test data. The game is to select which ad performs best in generating recall and persuasion among consumers in the target audience.

We say we play the game occasionally because it is so frustrating! Not for us, but for the entrepreneurs, because while they have tremendous energy and instincts, these qualities can only take one so far unless combined with a lot of experience. Everyone needs a healthy combination of intuition and actual data—that is, an educated intuition. In the ad-pair game, people often ignore the rules of thumb and the data and go with their gut. Predictably, the untrained gut sends them in the wrong direction nearly every time! Then

BOOM
THOUGHT 1.1

The insight gained from simple, straightforward, and well-designed voice-of-the-customer research trumps "gut feel" every time!

they argue with us, the test data, and the testing procedure, and unfortunately continue to ignore the simple insights gleaned from decades of research data.

For example, imagine two print ads for shoes. The first ad has a big picture of a shoe with the headline "The Look That Never Wears Out" written beneath the brand name of the manufacturer. The other ad shows a very attractive woman gazing eagerly at a well-dressed man wearing the manufacturer's shoes, walking away from her, with the headline "Anytime, Anyplace, Anywhere" prominently displayed over the brand name of the manufacturer. If we want to sell shoes, which ad do you feel is the more effective—the first print ad or the second? Gut feel often directs people to the second ad. After all, there is a sexy woman in the second ad and everyone knows that "sex sells." However, in practice the second ad performs poorly, because consumers are busy people, too busy to figure out that the sexy woman is actually selling shoes. On the other hand, the first ad performs well above norm for the category because it is obvious to even busy consumers what is being sold. By the numbers, the first ad generates 21% recall of ad and advertiser, whereas the second ad manages only 6% recall, less than half of the 15% recall that is the category norm.

Some people prefer to trust their gut and learn from their own hard-knock experiences. Some people prefer to train their gut by learning from the experience of others. We prefer the latter and hope you will too!

Market vs. Marketing Research

Market research and marketing research are two different things, but admittedly it is easy to get them confused. Many dictionaries even list them as synonyms, but we think you'll agree with us that there are some important distinctions that once understood, make us better users of both. Market research helps us understand the demographics of a marketplace—that is, how many people buy, how much people buy, how much people pay, what kind of people buy, which brands perform the best, and what the potential is for new growth or new brands. In contrast, marketing research tells us how to effectively position, promote, design, distribute, and price our products once we've decided on a market.

Entrepreneurs most often are interested in market research and not marketing research. They want to find the so-called "low-hanging fruit," i.e., a marketplace with tremendous growth potential for their particular product idea—a large market where their product will sell itself. Unfortunately, finding low-hanging fruit is more like finding a needle in a haystack. Consider the story of Kevlar, which *Fortune* magazine aptly described as a "miracle in search of a market." Kevlar was developed by DuPont decades ago as a replacement for fiberglass tire cord. Turns out steel worked better. Now DuPont had a $400 million Kevlar plant to fill and no market to supply. Like Moses in the wilderness, DuPont managers have searched and searched for the promised land of economic milk and honey. Bulletproof vests, military helmets, golf equipment, loudspeaker cones, tennis racket frames, substitutes for steel-wire rope, etc., all added up to less than a handful of grapes! DuPont admits that if they'd simply put all of the money they invested in Kevlar in the bank, the interest earned would be greater than the profits gained from selling Kevlar products. Kevlar product managers just haven't been able to identify a market where mass quantities of Kevlar sell themselves.

Tyvek is another DuPont product. Early on, it was sold as a replacement for satin in "law tags," those pesky "do not remove this tag under penalty of law" tags found on pillows and mattresses. DuPont also tried selling Tyvek as mailing envelopes and large advertising banners for stores and businesses, but it wasn't until they found a marketing angle with Tyvek Housewrap that they really stumbled on a winner to fill the capacity of their manufacturing plants. Company literature states that Tyvek Housewrap "acts like a windbreaker" for your home, "resisting air infiltration and water intrusion, making for a more comfortable, energy-efficient home or building." Now we are talking! Let's wrap every new house and building in the modern world with a Tyvek "windbreaker." And to give the new construction a finished and professional look, let's sell an entire weatherization system consisting of wrap, flashing, wrap caps, and tape, and make Tyvek wrap thick enough so that it won't rip in the wind. With Tyvek Housewrap, DuPont managers went after a large market—they'd done their market research on new housing starts—and added in a moderate dose of marketing research to optimize product positioning, promotion, pricing, and profitable product development ideas. These managers made the most of Tyvek's sales potential by stressing marketing research right along with market research. They never expected Tyvek to sell itself. Rather than letting Tyvek be a "miracle in search of a market," they used smart research to find ways to make the market search for the Tyvek miracle.

Making Fast Decisions Good Decisions!

Entrepreneurs live in a fast-paced world where decisions must be made quickly. We don't have a problem with fast! As we work with new businesses, there are few things we see more frustrating than paralysis by analysis. Get out there and start doing! If you want to learn how to sell something, get out there and start selling it! If you don't sell anything, start asking questions. Find out what works well enough to create some interest, yet not quite well enough to generate sales. Trial and error can be one of the best ways to gather data and acquire the educated intuition we all strive for.

BOOM
THOUGHT 1.2

Ignoring timely customer feedback is a sure way to slow down the forward progress of your startup.

John Kilcullen writes that ignoring early customer data was his biggest mistake in developing the wildly successful *For Dummies* book series. Even though the early books used "bounce back" cards to gather customer data, the information was set aside and not compiled to help the new business better appreciate buying motives and emotional attachments to the books. Mr. Kilcullen admits[3] that seven out of the first nine books in the *For Dummies* series were commercial failures. He warns, "We might have had success with the first book and saved hundreds of thousands of dollars in unnecessary costs if we'd done prepublication research to sharpen our focus. Even if we had used our data more wisely during those early years, we might have developed new products more efficiently and achieved more cost-effective and targeted direct marketing."

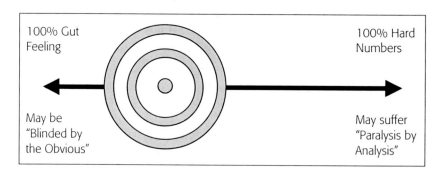

Similar to the figure shown above, we believe that successful entrepreneurs are guided more by gut than "100% hard numbers." Good business decisions don't require millions of dollars of quantitative research, but they do require open eyes and ears. In fact, we

---

[3]"John J. Kilcullen: My Biggest Mistake," in *Inc. Magazine* (May 2000)

have seen companies do millions of dollars of research just to leave the results gathering dust on shelves. In truth, there is often good, ample, and easily obtained information all around us to give entrepreneurs a sense of whether or not they are moving in the right direction. But good information is easy to ignore. We love the passion entrepreneurs put into their ideas, but sometimes this passion gives them made-by-me myopia. It leaves them blinded by the obvious. Of course, non-entrepreneurs can fall into the same trap. We learned the term "blinded by the obvious" from a creative director at a local advertising agency. In his tenure at the ad agency, advertisers consistently made so many obvious errors in their advertising copy and media expenditures that he coined the term to describe the phenomenon. In short, advertisers get so enamored with their advertising idea, approach, goal, or media choice that all reason and perspective go right out the window and mistakes are made that even the casual observer could catch. To help a new concept take flight, we need to answer the question "What does this product promise?" and then start doing everything we can to deliver on that promise. Once we lose our focus on the product promise, it is easy to get off track.

For example, consider the advertiser that decided far too many poor-quality sales leads were being generated by their advertising campaign. In response to the concern, the single-minded message of the new campaign veered away from the "product promise" in favor of filtering out poor-quality sales leads. Very little thought was given to how well the new advertising sold the actual product or what the ultimate impact of the filtering effort would be.

The resulting campaign left viewers unclear as to what, if anything was being sold by the advertising. The ads, however, did prove to be a powerful filter. Sales leads were reduced by a factor of ten, i.e., 50,000 sales leads per month declined to 5,000 per month. Unfortunately, the new sales leads were not any more productive than the old sales leads. Ouch! The advertiser's single-minded focus on filtering sales leads blinded them to some facts obvious to everyone except the advertiser: (1) advertising first and foremost must highlight the product promise and explain how the product delivers on that promise, and (2) the fewer the sales leads, the fewer the sales.

One Inquiring Mind Is Worth More Than a Company-Load of Consultants

In his book *Art of Problem Solving*, Wharton Professor Emeritus Russell Ackoff tells a story about an oil company that was trying to unravel the secret of making their gasoline stations more profitable. As large companies will do, the oil company hired an expensive group of consultants. The consultants collected data, and lots of it. They assembled information on dozens of variables from hundreds of gasoline stations, and then used a statistical model to relate these variables to station profitability. The model identified the variables that exerted the greatest influence on profit. Back in the day, a pretty impressive feat, but today most MBA graduates from competent programs can do this analysis blindfolded—and from what we've seen, they might just as well be blindfolded.

The oil company was pleased with the research and quickly moved to implement the research findings. Unfortunately, the changes they made did not significantly improve station profitability. You see, the wrong kind of research can also cause paralysis— profit paralysis, that is! Smart research trumps "gut feel," but gut feel trumps misguided research. Collecting more and more data rarely leads to making better and better decisions. Just collect what you will use. Anything more will often just blind and confuse.

In the case of gasoline station profitability, one bright person with an inquiring mind asked the oil company for a list of very profitable and a list of very unprofitable stations. He then visited the profitable and unprofitable stations and opened his eyes and ears. What he saw and heard was that people were concerned about getting in and out of the gas station as easily and quickly as possible. The profitable stations satisfied these needs. The unprofitable stations did not. The recommendations were simple: Locate the stations so that traffic patterns and traffic lights make it easy to quickly get in and out of the station. Americans are not a patient bunch. Anything to make the fueling faster and more convenient will increase profitability. As you might expect, the simple, smart research from one inquiring mind paid off generously for the oil company.

Yes, in some cases we still need to collect data and do some analysis. However, we recommend that you keep things simple. Avoid "black-box" models. Stay personally involved in the information gathering. Don't fall so far in love with your own ideas that the key point, making profitable sales, gets lost in the shuffle.

Chase Customers, Not Competitors

To achieve breakthrough success, entrepreneurs must carve out new space in the market, redraw the competitive map, and rethink the marketing concept. Chasing customers and not competitors is at the very core of having the right stuff!

BOOM

─── THOUGHT 1.3 ───

Big competitors set the bar for what customers believe they need and want in terms of product features and benefits. To win, startups must play to strength and redefine the rules of the game.

Entrepreneurs face a David and Goliath competitive environment. Established competitors have more of everything: more money, more marketplace experience, more name recognition, more distribution, and more customers. The Goliath wields so much power as to even set the benchmark for what customers believe they need and want in terms of product features and benefits. The Goliath defines the competitive landscape, chooses the weapons, and picks the battles in a way that plays to their strength.

In such a world, how is little David supposed to compete, much less win? Certainly, David will not succeed by playing the same game as Goliath. If David straps on some oversized armor, picks out a heavy sword and shield, and puts on a huge helmet, Goliath is sure to strike him down. To have a fighting chance, David needs to play to his own unique set of strengths, even if the casual onlooker is initially unimpressed. He must do it like the defiant underdog rebel he is.

Consider the 1980s case study of Xerox, a true Goliath, and Canon, the upstart David. Xerox dominated business copying. Perhaps you remember going into the centralized copy room before a big meeting needing some copies of your presentation, waiting in line, and then having the big Xerox copy machine break down halfway through the project. To anyone caring to notice, it seemed like there was some vulnerability to exploit, and companies such as IBM and Kodak tried to do it. They built big copiers of their own and went toe-to-toe with Xerox. But Xerox was, after all, the Goliath, and easily handled everything IBM and Kodak sent their way.

IBM and Kodak just couldn't beat Xerox at the centralized copier game. If someone was going to defeat Goliath, they needed to find something new and different, and then teach customers to get excited about it.

Along came Canon, just a little David in the copier market with little toy-like copiers. Xerox executives and engineers laughed at Canon's pathetic product offerings. After all, Canon was not even competing for the centralized copier business. Canon was pushing something called distributed copying—that is, small copiers distributed to individual offices and departments that were highly reliable and available for making copies when you really needed them, just before the big meeting. Sure, in the early days the copy speed and quality produced by Canon wasn't as good as the big Xerox, but the speed and quality were more than adequate for the front-line user.

Canon educated office managers and front-line users on the advantages of their little copiers, bypassing the traditional purchasing department selling channel that was locked up by Xerox. Front-line users educated their bosses and the bosses authorized purchases. People stopped using the big Xerox, except when quality really mattered and time really didn't. The sales of Xerox consumables like paper, toner, and service declined dramatically. Canon changed the rules of the game, and Xerox was brought to its knees, taking a decade to recover. Xerox, as the Goliath, had many advantages, but one deadly disadvantage. Like all well-known brands, Xerox had a well-defined image and way of doing business that it could not walk away from. Xerox was trapped by its own success— brought down by its own powerful sword. Entrepreneurial products don't carry baggage. They have the freedom to compete and win by following their own path to success and building on their unique customer-must-have qualities.

Be the Market Driver, Not Market-Driven

Market-driving strategies[4] are particularly effective when creating a new-to-the-world market for a new-to-the-world product. With market-driving strategies, entrepreneurs have the freedom and flex-

---

[4]"Market-Driving Strategies: Toward a New Concept of Competitive Advantage," by Carpenter, Glazer, and Nakamoto, in *Kellogg on Marketing* (2000)

ibility to observe the problems customers are having with competitive products and then introduce new products to address clumsy workarounds and other latent needs. New technology can often be the key to solving old problems.

From the Xerox-Canon case study, Canon marketers were able to tap into latent needs by offering copy machines that were small, reliable, and available rather than big, fast, and pretty. Customers can be so entrenched in personal workarounds that innovative solutions often require innovative selling. Canon aggressively reeducated customers about the *ideal copier*, redrew the competitive landscape, and succeeded by inventing their own version of the marketing concept. At the time, Canon's Japanese executives hadn't read the marketing textbooks popular at American business schools. They didn't know about the marketing concept. They only knew how to make and sell new products.

We have now all heard of the marketing concept. In a nutshell, it is all about listening to what people say they want, and then realigning our business resources to give people what they want better than the competition. On paper, the marketing concept sounds like a winner. How can you go wrong if you give people what they want? In practice, however, the trouble is that most people rearrange their lives and ways of thinking to want what the marketplace Goliath offers. Marketing is primarily an imitative process and not an innovative process. The Goliath sets the benchmark and draws the battle lines for how people view and evaluate new products.

BOOM
THOUGHT 1.4

New technology is not a product until an entrepreneur makes it a solution. New technology often is the key to solving old problems.

Market-driven entrepreneurs in love with the marketing concept hand Goliath an unfair advantage. Like IBM and Kodak challenging Xerox, they are beaten before they ever get started. To break the Goliath advantage, *market-driving* entrepreneurs take advantage of their small size and marketing freedom and change the rules for winning by raising the relevance of the product features and benefits they uniquely own. Entrepreneurs must assess what they can do best, play to strength in addressing below-the-surface *latent needs*, and then enthusiastically teach customers to love their new solution.

In many US companies, we have something called "me-too" marketing. This marketing approach delivers products that say, "I'm just as good as," or "I'm just as good as and cost less." Everyone will tell you that "me-too" marketing is the bane of new products. Research shows that "me-too" marketing is one of the top reasons new products fail. To succeed, products must stand for something different that is important. Being a *market driver* is the only way for entrepreneurs to avoid "me-too" marketing. We can only stand for something different that is important when we teach people why it is important to buy and own a product that stands for something different.

Entrepreneurs can sidestep "me-too" marketing by rethinking the marketing concept. Rather than using a questionnaire to ask what customers want and then giving it to them better than the competition, we suggest using your own eyes to carefully observe the latent needs of customers, using your unique strengths to satisfy those latent needs, and creating a new market space. The only way to be a market driver is to create a new market space. Anything less is being market-driven, which is to say, driven by the marketplace Goliath to be a niche player if allowed to play at all.

Raising the Relevance Bar

Anyone who has ever been around teenagers knows that you can't convince someone that something is relevant or important just by saying that it is! Raising the relevance bar requires real ingenuity. Playing to strength is one thing, but making that strength important to people demands that we develop a knack for recognizing pain and then learn how to make connections between our unique solution for that pain and the human emotions that energize our lives. Said another way, we have to connect product, pain, and person.

Values research provides a roadmap or ladder that shows us how to connect product, pain, and person. Marketers find it useful for developing market-driving advertising and marketing approaches[5] that raise the relevance bar.

Products struggle when they don't find a way of making the right emotional connection with people. For example, let's say that

---

[5] "Applying Laddering Data to Communications Strategy and Advertising Practice," by Reynolds and Whitlark, in *Journal of Advertising Research* (1995)

you have invested big money in developing an electrically powered, self-balancing, computer-controlled two-wheeled vehicle on which people can stand up and ride. There has never been a vehicle quite like it. It is so revolutionary that no one can even figure out what to call it. You name it the Segway Scooter. In the first year, you plan on selling between 50,000 and 100,000 vehicles. However, over the first 21 months you sell only about 6,000. People's emotional reactions to the scooter are mixed. It looks cool and futuristic. Users say that people always stop you and want to talk about it.

BOOM
THOUGHT 1.5

Many good products struggle for years before finding a market. Even innovative products must make the right emotional connection with people in order to succeed.

On the other hand, people often feel foolish when riding it, and after President George Bush's well-publicized fall from a Segway, they feel a little uncertain about their personal safety. So with the Segway, the revolutionary $5,000 commuter vehicle, what do we have? It is a vehicle that attracts the sort of attention that slows you down, makes you feel conspicuous and foolish, and raises concerns about personal safety. With commuters the Segway makes an emotional connection, but not a very positive one! It creates pain rather than alleviating it.

There must be a way for the Segway to solve some pain and make a positive emotional connection. For the *trained rider*, they are fast, maneuverable, reduce personal fatigue, and put you head and shoulders above the crowd. Who would get some emotional bang out of those sorts of product features and benefits? Would you believe the police? Segways were adopted by the German police in February 2006 and were put in full service for police officers patrolling Chicago's O'Hare International Airport in February 2004. Officers are thrilled because the Segway enables them to do more of what they enjoy about their jobs: being visible, finding lost children, addressing security threats, and quickly covering vast distances without arousing suspicion or concern. Running police officers freak people out, whereas two officers riding Segways only attract glances of admiration and interest. Riding Segways gives the police at O'Hare Airport feelings of efficiency, productivity, confidence, and accomplishment. Now, that is a positive emotional connection!

Understanding customer pain, values, and how they connect with product features and benefits can go a long way in making your product offering relevant and important. Sometimes we need to find a new set of customers in order to make the connection. Sometimes we just need to understand a little bit more about the pain of our current customers.

Brand Champions Are the Key to Finding the Right Emotional Connection

Brand champions have the information you need to push forward your ideas in the marketplace. When someone enthusiastically responds to your new product idea, talk to them and find out everything you can about the love, because it is the key to understanding the emotional connection between product, pain, and person. There is a three-step research process to help you in the quest. It goes by the general name of values research, and consists of eliciting distinctions, pyramiding down, and laddering up. It is a straightforward process,[6] but it does require some patience and your keen interest in understanding customer pain, your product, and the love that binds product to person.

Picking an example many people can relate to, we'll ladder and pyramid the world's number one soda drink, Coca-Cola, using a hypothetical respondent, Martin. The first step is to elicit product distinctions by listing several popular brands of soft drinks, including Coca-Cola, and then asking Martin to put the brands in rank order from the one consumed most often to the one consumed least often. You can make the exercise even more interesting by referencing a particular situation, such as "when spending time with friends." Let's say that the result of the ordering exercise is shown below, e.g., Coca-Cola is consumed by Martin most often when spending time with friends.

1. Coca-Cola
2. Sprite
3. 7-Up
4. Orange Crush
5. Barq's Root Beer

---

[6] "Advancements in Laddering," by Reynolds, Dethloff, and Westberg, in *Understanding Consumer Decision Making: The Means-End Approach to Marketing and Advertising Strategy* (2001)

6. Stewart's Grape Soda
7. Pepsi-Cola

With the ordered list in hand, we want to find out which product distinctions elevate Coca-Cola to the top spot. So we ask Martin another simple question: "What are some reasons you drink Coca-Cola more often than the other sodas when spending time with friends?" These "reasons for" are called product distinctions. The distinctions are listed below for our sample interviewee.

a) I like the taste
b) It is a tradition
c) It adds to the fun
d) Friends all like it
e) It goes best with snacks

Next, we ask Martin which reason, of the five listed, is the most important reason he drinks Coca-Cola more often than other sodas when spending time with friends. Let's say his answer is "Friends all like it."

The next step in the process is pyramiding down from the most important distinction, "Friends all like it." We ask another straightforward question: "What is it about drinking Coca-Cola that you and your friends like?" We follow up with similar probing questions to add as much detail to the "pyramid" supporting the prod-

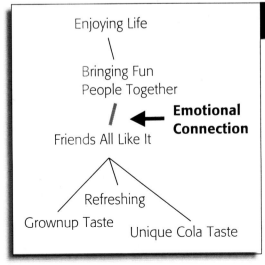

Values Research Uncovers the "Love Connection"

Product strengths only become relevant and important when they make a positive connection with our emotions. Look to brand champions to find the connection.

uct benefit as possible. Pyramiding uncovers the distinctively good attributes of a product. For this product, consumers like Martin may respond with attributes like great taste, unique cola taste, taste we have grown up with, refreshing taste, not too sweet, grownup taste, etc.

The last step in the process is laddering up from the most important distinction while reminding the interviewee about the situation and supporting attributes. These questions are more complex and require considerable patience on the part of interviewer and interviewee. Don't jump to easy answers, because laddering reveals the product-person connection we desperately need to know. To "ladder up," we first put the person in the situation by saying, "Think for a moment about the last time you were drinking Coca-Cola with your friends. Tell me about that last time!" After listening to the response, we then continue by asking, "What is it about everyone enjoying Coca-Cola in that situation that you find satisfying and meaningful?" After asking this question, we sit back and listen, encouraging the interviewee to elaborate with phrases like "On a personal level, what does that mean to you," "Tell me more about those feelings," and "Please go on." Laddering uncovers personal evaluations, moods, strong feelings, emotions, and the personal values that give them power. Take the time to interview 10 to 15 brand champions. We know you will be rewarded with the keys to connect your product with the marketplace.

Perfecting the planning and execution of values research can be a study in itself, but eager entrepreneurs willing to ask the few questions listed above can get surprisingly far on their own. Ultimately, we want to uncover the emotional connection, the "Love Connection," that our product makes with people who love our product. That emotional connection, called the "personal relevance bridge" in values research, provides a deep understanding of the "product promise" and the leverage we need to raise the relevance of our product strengths and pursue a successful market-driving strategy.

Turning the Right Stuff into Green Stuff

Entrepreneurial marketing is *marketing on a shoestring*. There are no big budgets, no fancy offices, and no high-priced marketing consultants. Only spend a dollar to make two dollars or don't spend at all. Referring to out-of-control spending in the US Congress, Senator Everett Dickerson is quoted as saying, "A billion here, a billion there, pretty soon it adds up to real money." The same can be said for spending on ineffective marketing or any other low-leveraged spending in a startup business. Regardless of the quality of our startup idea, to be successful we must make it a point to live by this mantra: *Only spend a dollar to make two dollars or don't spend at all.*

Your startup may be oozing with the right stuff, but it takes discipline to turn revenue into profit. In the early critical months of a new business, it is not unusual for us to see entrepreneurs upside down in their day-to-day cash flows—that is, spending two dollars in labor and material costs for every dollar of revenue they bring in. Usually that problem can be fixed if the entrepreneurs see it soon enough, but far too many entrepreneurs get caught up in the dream of building a business, ignore the cost problem, and then throw crazy money at a wild effort to bring in more customers to boost revenue. We've seen startups blow an entire marketing budget on a single PR stunt or a few broadcast TV or cable ads, or pour money down the drain by putting complex and ill-conceived messages on a few billboards in order to do something to "save" the business.

BOOM
THOUGHT 1.6

Traditional marketing is getting more expensive and less effective all the time. Most entrepreneurs might as well burn their money for all the good it does on TV ads, 2-for-1 giveaways, and billboards.

It is human nature to get caught up in building the dream and forget that the dream must pay the bills and feed the family. All startups teeter on the edge of disaster, and spending marketing dollars haphazardly like a drunken sailor or even methodically like a deep-pocket Fortune 500 company won't help matters any.

Get Big Fast and Other Myths

The need for embracing our "spend a dollar to make two dollars" mantra is easy enough to accept, yet it is so hard not to spend like one of the big boys. There is no better example of this phenomenon than the dot-com theory of *get large or get lost*. In the years leading up to the dot-com bubble burst, Internet entrepreneurs came to believe that their survival depended on big-scale marketing to grow their customer base as rapidly as possible. This marketers-gone-wild mindset came to a head when 17 dot-com companies spent upwards of $100 million to produce and air ads during Super Bowl XXXIV. Investors had speculated that big dot-com revenues would translate into big dot-com profits, but flagging revenues and nonexistent profits in the wake of the so-called dot-com Super Bowl convinced even the most optimistic that no amount of capital could keep up with over-the-top burn rates of Internet startups.

Pets.com is the poster child for failing to turn the right stuff into green stuff. In a short nine months, the company went from $80 million IPO to pennies-on-the-dollar liquidation. The company started with a glitzy regional advertising campaign covering TV, print, and radio. They then went national with crowd-pleasing Super Bowl ads. The nameless Pets.com sock puppet featured in the marketing campaign became a national pop icon. The company stood out from the crowd. However, the revenue breakeven point for the business was estimated at an astounding $300 million, and in the months it operated, Pets.com only generated revenues of around $45 million. From IPO to liquidation, the company lost over $3 million a month, and when the doors closed, investors received just 17 cents on the dollar. Analysts summed up the failure by saying, "You can't build a brand with a bad business plan." Building brand awareness as an antecedent to sales is still very important, but Old School marketing is far too expensive for startup businesses.

Pinch every penny is another myth for new businesses. We encourage entrepreneurs to spend highly leveraged dollars and not to scrimp. It's great to spend a dollar as long as you receive two dollars in return! Being generous is an important aspect of making money. Observing successful and unsuccessful businesses, we see the successful ones being generous with customer service, product consultation, and product upgrades. The successful are generous with the value they create and always looking for new ways to add value. Consequently, generous startup businesses build a very loyal love group, which spreads a positive and compelling marketing message more effectively than a TV ad ever could.

BOOM
THOUGHT 1.7

Measurement is the key to finding the type of marketing expenditures that do the most good for your product, market, and set of competitors.

Measure the Leverage

How can you tell whether the marketing cost is worth the marketing benefit? We recommend measuring the direct effects of any marketing dollars you spend. Big business engages in a lot of what is called "awareness and image" advertising. Measuring its effect is difficult. To make the measurement, one needs to benchmark existing levels of awareness and brand image with a regional or national survey, spend megabucks on an advertising campaign, and then re-measure awareness and brand attitudes. Analysts then look for statistically significant differences. However, even if the analysts find statistically significant differences, it does not mean they are finding financially significant differences. Believing that improved awareness and image leads to a better bottom line is a logical leap of faith, but a leap of faith nonetheless.

To measure the leverage of our startup marketing dollars, we must set aside "awareness and image" advertising and take a tip from direct marketers. Direct marketers embed a call to action in every bit of marketing they do. Including a coupon, website, phone number, free gift, etc., in the marketing communications allows managers to count results in people, sales leads, and revenue dollars. This approach presumes the communications channel and marketing piece are well enough selected to improve awareness and image, and turns the attention towards financial results. "Right stuff" entrepreneurs must be direct marketers. Explore multiple communications channels. Test multiple marketing pieces. Stick with the ones that produce the best results and when generating new ideas use the tried and true approaches as the benchmark.

Break the Money Barrier

Money is the most obvious barrier to entrepreneurship. To get started, we must find a way to feed the family, make the house payment, and fund a business without raining down irreversible financial ruin on us and our loved ones. For most people, the *money barrier* is the single most petrifying proposition of entrepreneurship. But successful entrepreneurs will tell you that while it is the most obvious, money is not the biggest barrier. We know of entrepreneurs who have creatively financed their way into wildly successful startup businesses with less than $10,000 out-of-pocket. The least obvious, but biggest barrier is learning how to identify and spend highly leveraged marketing dollars.

Knowing what constitutes a highly leveraged marketing dollar will differ based upon the product, market, and set of competitors. With Old School marketing, advertising is the one-size-fits-all solution. However, for today's startup businesses there is no such thing as one-size-fits-all. For example, money spent on search engine optimization (SEO), giveaway promotions, and careful website design may be highly leveraged marketing dollars for an Internet-based software business. On the other hand, for a craft-oriented business, spending money to organize marketing events at local shopping centers may be what is needed. To find the highly leveraged dollars, we need to try a lot of ideas and measure the results.

Success Is Ahead

"Right stuff" ideas are right in front of us. Remember that better than two out of three successful startups are based on good ol' entrepreneurial R&D—that is, ripping off, designing, and improving upon a good idea encountered through previous employment—and that two out of ten successful startups result via serendipitous discovery from being ultra-observant. Successful entrepreneurs don't need to have a huge war chest of money, but do need to keep their eyes open and work at being smart observers. Successful entrepreneurs look for problems and ways to solve them. They know that (1) nobody pays to solve a non-problem and (2) non-solutions to real problems quickly fail under the intense pressures of a competitive marketplace.

Over the years, we've identified laws and their consequences that entrepreneurs new and old have found particularly helpful when launching their "right stuff" ideas. Over the next five chapters, we share what we have learned and pieced together: (1) sharpen the angle, (2) ride horses, (3) play big, (4) do an event, and (5) reap the rewards. We call what we have found "SuperLaws" because each law encompasses many overlapping thoughts, best practices, and tips for turning your startup dream into a booming marketplace reality.

Review Questions

Define with Five

Define the following vocabulary words using five words or less.

1. Entrepreneurial R&D

_____

2. Low-Hanging Fruit

_____

3. Be a David to their Goliath

_____

4. Market-Driving Products

_____

5. Values Research Map

_____

Question the Answer

Answer each phrase below in the form of a question.

1. Why this, why now, why here, and why you?

_____

2. The product characteristic that elevates a new venture from copy-cat to unique and valued.

_____

3. Sharpen the angle, ride horses, play big, throw an event, and reap the rewards.

_____

4. Research describing how many people buy, how much people buy, and how much people pay.

_____

5. Marketing that says, "I'm just as good and cost less."

_____

Smarter than an Entrepreneur

Name the product or venture that reinforces or violates a Boom Start best practice.

1. The venture had an inexperienced business team and asked for millions of dollars without providing any hard numbers showing customer demand, revenue, or breakeven points.

_____

2. A product that was called "a miracle in search of a market."

_____

3. A product that failed seven out of nine times because while customer feedback was collected, it was ignored.

_____

4. A revolutionary product that when it was launched, created more pain than it solved.

_____

5. A venture that was a poster child for the "get large or get lost" startup myth.

_____

SuperLaws in Action

Many believe that entrepreneurs are born with an extra-big dose of creativity. On the other hand, Google's Marissa Mayer asserts that "creativity loves constraint." In this activity, we'll put both ideas to the test. Is creativity a gift given to only a chosen few, or is creativity in the grasp of everyone if they simply put some constraints around the problem?

Activity: Use a ball to develop a new product idea. The ball can be big or small, hard or soft, colorful or plain.

INSERT A DRAWING
OF THE PRODUCT

27

Describe the product and how it will be used:

Describe who will purchase and use the product:

Describe the usage situations for the product:

What price will you charge for the product?

About how many units of the product will you sell in your first year?

Sharpen the Angle

Entrepreneurs are by nature optimistic and believe they have a unique idea that the world has never seen and everyone will want to buy. However, experience shows that uniqueness does not come easily and must be earned by sharpening the angle.

Big business loves strategy. We love strategy too, but entrepreneurs love competitive angles. Indeed, we'd say that entrepreneurs are obsessed with competitive angles! In our experience, we have seen that the choice of competitive angle is what really determines winners and losers. Great products and great startups have great competitive angles. When aspiring entrepreneurs come our way and ask us to evaluate their latest big idea, the first thing we look for is the competitive angle. Inexperienced entrepreneurs often don't think in terms of competitive angle. For us the most important task within entrepreneurial marketing is to identify, nurture, and sharpen the angle.

Jack Trout in his book *Differentiate or Die* defines a competitive angle as an "element of differentness," such as "smaller, big-

Pinggg . . . That's an Angle

Spare-time golfer Karsten Solheim re-invented the putter in 1959. It looked different from other putters because of its perimeter "heel-toe" weighting, and unlike other putters, made a "musical" ping sound when striking a golf ball squarely.

ger, lighter, heavier, cheaper or more expensive," and notes that winning products must have one. Mr. Trout is absolutely right; successful entrepreneurs, however, have found that a competitive angle can be so much more than some simple point of difference. To capture the thinking of hall-of-fame entrepreneurs, we divide up the notion of competitive angle into five different factors or di-mensions. These are (1) need to believe, (2) reason to believe, (3) blows away expectations, (4) quantifiable support, and (5) unique product claim. At first blush, most fledgling entrepreneurs believe their competitive angle has all of these qualities, but after digging deeper and doing a little soul-searching, soon they discover that most every competitive angle can be sharpened and improved. We hope that you will start to see what is possible for your own startup idea as we talk through Karsten Solheim's classic example.

Back in 1959, when Karsten Solheim introduced his first Ping putter to the golfing world, golf clubs, and particularly putters, all looked very much the same. One might describe putters back in that era as narrow slabs of rough-hewn metal hanging at the end of crude shafts topped with clumsy leather grips. At the time, putter sales were dominated by three large companies: Wilson, Spalding, and Acushnet. Because of the sharpness of Karsten Solheim's competitive angle, only one of these companies is still a major player in manufacturing putters, and that company primarily sells highly refined and expensive versions of original Karsten designs.

> # BOOM
> ## THOUGHT 2.1
>
> *Startups must find a competitive angle that passes the litmus test. Is your angle red or blue? How does it score on uniqueness, believability, and customer value?*

Before the Ping putter, golfing heroes such as Arnold Palmer and Jack Nicklaus managed to use the aforementioned primitive putters to sink long putts and win big tournaments, but for most of us, trying to sink a good-sized putt with one of these off-balance, easily twisted, Neanderthal-like weapons was little more than a futile exercise in pain and frustration. Mr. Solheim, engineer and spare-time golfer, also must have felt the pain. His answer was an odd-looking device that removed weight from the middle of the clubface and piled it up on the heel and toe of the putter.

The *need to believe* among golfers that there is a superior putter is a powerful force. Back then and even today, millions of golfers need to believe there is a solution for their bad putting and want to believe that perimeter "heel-toe" weighting will work magic. The weight distribution of a Ping putter is meant to keep the clubface from twisting so that it is easy to hit the putt straight and presumably make more putts. The Ping putter measurably reduced twisting by 50%. No other putter at the time could make that claim of *quantifiable support* for improving the putter design, and even though it looked pretty strange to golfers when it was first introduced, it certainly looked like it should work. Mr. Solheim also put a bend in the club's hosel to make hits with the putter feel solid and positioned a long slot in the bottom of the clubhead parallel to the clubface that made the putter "pinggg" when golfers hit the ball squarely. Ping's "music" gave golfers feedback and confidence that it was doing its job, and greater confidence often results in better putting, as golf is primarily played in those six inches between our ears.

Karsten Solheim's Ping putter, whether by plan or by serendipity, has every factor of the angle expertly covered. He ran the business out of his garage for seven years, but Karsten's company now manufactures many of the world's most loved golfing products and has grown to about 1,000 employees working in dozens of buildings. The "perimeter weighting" competitive angle started with putters but soon grew into a full line of Ping golf clubs, creating a new category of "game improvement" golf clubs that have dominated the world market for 20 years and counting. In the words of John Solheim, Karsten's son, "If you're just a 'me-too,' then you're not leading."

Litmus Test

Litmus is a blue substance found naturally in plants that changes to red with increasing acidity and back to blue with increasing basicity. Red competitive angles are losers and eat holes in pockets and poison startups. Blue competitive angles are winners and score well on all five factors: need to believe, reason to believe, blows away expectations, quantifiable support, and unique product claim. Does your competitive angle pass the litmus test? Let's learn to apply it by considering how the Ping putter scores. We don't want to get overly analytical, so let's use a simple three-category rating system: red (no), yellow (can't decide), and blue (yes).

Does the pain of putting give golfers *need to believe*? Blue, because of the burning-hot pain of missed putts; golfers are on a never-ending quest for the magic club that will make it easier to putt the ball into the hole. With putters and golfers, there was and still is a strong *need to believe*. Does the Ping putter have *reason to believe*? Blue, because of the way the club looks with weight piled up on both sides of the clubface; it suggests a physical reason that the clubhead will twist less than the conventional putters of the day. Does it *blow away expectations*? Blue; golfers expected the putter to twist less than other putters, but the Ping also felt solid, gave a pleasing "pinggg" sound when hit squarely, built confidence, and most importantly, made more putts. The Ping putter far exceeded the expectations of how a putter could perform. Does Ping's performance have *quantifiable support*? Blue, because in addition to the immediate feedback of sound and feel, Karsten also provided test results showing that the putter twisted 50% less during the putting stroke than conventional putters. Does everything add up to a *unique product claim* for Ping? Blue; because of the unsolved pain in the marketplace, the perimeter weighting and pleasing "pinggg" feedback of a perfect stroke, the ability for the average golfer to sink more putts, and the measurable resistance to twisting, the Ping had a uniqueness that no other club at the time could claim.

Passing the Litmus Test

FACTOR	PROOF STATEMENT
Need to Believe	Is there enough pain or opportunity to make people pull out their credit cards and buy?
Reason to Believe	Does the product "touch the human sense of believability" with a compelling proof-point?
Blows-Away Expectations	Does the product dominate a situation and deliver superior value?
Quantifiable Support	Are there relevant facts and figures to support and enhance product claims?
Unique Product Claim	Does the product earn its way into occupying a unique position in a customer's mind?

BIGFOOT Pizza

It is easy to fall in love with our own ideas, and because of their "can do" attitude, entrepreneurs often have a hard time seeing the faults in their big ideas. To help you learn how to judge between good and bad, between blue and red, consider the failure of the BIGFOOT Pizza in contrast to Ping's success.

In 1993 Pizza Hut introduced the BIGFOOT Pizza, supported by a big $300 million advertising and promotional campaign. Pizza Hut marketing managers envisioned the BIGFOOT as a way to tap into the economy pizza market dominated by Little Caesars and as the next big thing for building revenues for the business. The BIGFOOT was two square feet of pizza cut into 21 slices. For a similar price and with a similar taste, Little Caesars offered two pizzas. Did the BIGFOOT have *need to believe*? Yellow; for most Americans there is some daily pain involved with feeding the family. Parents are always hoping for a cheap meal to satisfy the kids. However, the product category just doesn't carry the same amount of unsolved pain as does golf, for which a magical club or miracle swing tip are constant pursuits. Did it have *reason to believe*? Red, because although it was two square feet of pizza, it was still just one pizza. At the time, Little Caesars had a much stronger *reason to believe* in the economy-pizza category because it was selling two pizzas for the price of one. Did the BIGFOOT *blow away expectations*? Red, because it didn't taste better or have noticeably superior ingredients compared to Little Caesars. At best it met expectations for an economy pizza, and actually fell far short of expectations for many loyal Pizza Hut customers, which ultimately drove many brand champions away from the Pizza Hut brand. Did it have *quantifiable support*? Yellow; it was two square feet of pizza, but it was difficult for economy-buyers to see how that was better than two pizzas for the price of one. Did all this add up to a unique product claim for the BIGFOOT pizza? Red, because Little Caesars already offered a similar amount of pizza with a similar taste and at a similar price with a stronger *reason to believe*. BIGFOOT was a "me too" product, and a sad one at that.

BOOM
THOUGHT 2.2

Huge marketing budgets cannot compensate for a product that fails the litmus test. Not even $300 million could push BIGFOOT into the winner's circle.

To make a tragic marketing tale even more tragic, the launch of the BIGFOOT Pizza helped Little Caesars more than it helped Pizza Hut. Pizza Hut's advertising campaign looked so similar to ads Little Caesars would run that the Pizza Hut ads ended up driving customers to Little Caesars and spiking Little Caesars sales. Making matters even worse, Pizza Hut sales for their traditional higher-margin pizzas fell noticeably. BIGFOOT revenues couldn't compensate for lost higher-margin sales, much less make up the cost of the expensive marketing campaign. Pizza Hut quickly started looking for ways to kill the product.

Now why is this story relevant for entrepreneurs? Simply said, if a product launched by a national powerhouse with tons of brand equity and backed up by a $300 million marketing campaign won't work with a weak competitive angle, what chance will a startup have with little or no reputation, brand equity, or marketing budget and a weak competitive angle?

Finessing the Factors

By now it is pretty obvious that we really believe in the angle! Read on to learn about five best practices that will help you better understand each of the factors for sharpening the angle. These best practices associated with the first SuperLaw are (1) *find unsolved*

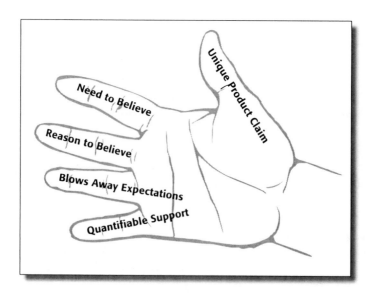

pain, which offers up some ways to find an idea with a strong *need to believe;* (2) *make the pitch,* which demonstrates how to highlight and amplify the *reason to believe;* (3) *dominate the situation,* which clarifies the relationship between customer value and customer expectations, and how to amplify customer value and *blow away expectations* by focusing the startup on dominating specific buying or usage situations; (4) *earn credibility, don't buy it,* which provides practical ideas on how to make support for product claims measurable, credible, and memorable; and (5) *hit the sweet spot,* which shows how to put it all together and turn a big idea into a *unique product claim* that connects with people.

Best Practice: Find Unsolved Pain

Psychologists and philosophers tell us there is a single driving force behind all human behavior. This powerful force impacts every aspect of our lives. Everything we do, the experts say, we do either out of our need to *avoid pain* or out of our eagerness to *pursue a great opportunity.* As an early example, in the 17th century, British philosopher John Locke argued that our natural inclination is to avoid pain and seek pleasure. It's hard to disagree with Mr. Locke!

We suspect that humans have been pain-avoiding opportunity-seekers for a long, long time. To avoid pain, our Stone Age cousins ran from the saber-toothed tiger. Today we run from inconvenience, anguish, distress, grief, embarrassment, discomfort, aging, hard work, etc., and we run toward fun, joy, gratification, satisfaction, good feelings, and the latest dieting fad. We constantly look for ways to reduce pain or add pleasure in our lives. And we are willing to pay for them! Think of the products you purchase. Why do you purchase them? Because they reduce some sort of unsolved pain in your life or they increase your opportunities for enjoyment. To sharpen the angle by giving it greater *need to believe,* we look for what hurts, irritates, bothers, annoys, and frustrates people and then provide a magical remedy or practical solution to stop the pain.

On the other hand, we find that people find enjoyment in the oddest things: a telephone molded into the shape of a cartoon character, tabloid magazines that publish stories about celebrity breakups and babies born with bat ears, bedtime slippers that look like bunny rabbits. Opportunity is about finding what enriches, gratifies, pleases, delights, enchants, and charms people. Perhaps the pursuit of opportunity is nothing more than soothing the pain of boredom, sameness, isolation, or feeling unfulfilled.

Risky Business

When consumers buy new products, they take risks. It's really quite remarkable, when you think about it, that any new product from any new venture actually succeeds. Some business studies we have seen suggest that the failure rate for new products is over 90%. Why in the world would anyone take the risk of trying a new product from a no-name entrepreneur when they could purchase existing products from well-known, established companies? The answer: the entrepreneur's product has a **relative advantage to reduce unsolved pain or deliver opportunity**.

Consumers see *relative advantage* when it is easy for them to understand how a product **reduces pain** or **delivers opportunity** in their day-to-day life situations. For example, cell phones keep us in touch without making us suffer the caged-in pain of being stuck at home or in the office. Reliable cars keep us on-the-go without making us suffer the crippling pain of frequent breakdowns and repairs. Audiobooks keep us up-to-date without making us suffer the laborious pain of having to read a dull book all by ourselves.

People Know How to Stop the Pain

When we experience pain, we look for ways to completely eliminate it. Consequently, the positive by-products of pain are creativity, inventiveness, and resourcefulness, because, let's be honest about it: we are totally desperate to find a way out. The Greek philosopher Plato[1] said it as well as anyone: "Necessity is the mother of invention." When we hurt, we seek relief and actively search for ways to take the pain away.

Similarly, Clayton Christensen of the Harvard Business School observes:

> *Customers are ingenious and inventive. When they have a job that needs to get done, they rarely let the job fester and languish,*

---

[1] *The New Dictionary of Cultural Literacy*

undone. They look around, find something that allows them to get by, and solve their problem. Often, they may not be solving the problem well—frequently they are not even aware of the awkward ways in which they have adapted products that had been designed for other purposes to do other jobs that needed to be done. [2]

Consider a simple product: sodium bicarbonate, also known as baking soda. For many of us, Arm & Hammer baking soda is the brand that comes to mind. For more than 160 years, the product has been a fixture in our homes. Originally designed for baking in 1846, the product's usages have grown considerably over time because consumers have found many new ways to use the product to reduce pain in their lives. Today we use the product for baking, cleaning (almost anything from microwave ovens to fresh fruits and vegetables to baby toys to the Statue of Liberty), deodorizing (refrigerators, freezers, carpets, upholstery, sink drains, retainers), washing (laundry), bathing, brushing, freshening, clearing (pool water), extinguishing (grease fires), calming (upset tummies), soaking (feet). Where did these usage ideas come from? Customers! Indeed, customers knew before the company that baking soda could be used to solve all sorts of problems and reduce pain for them. Today Arm & Hammer's website invites inventive customers to share their problem-solving tips under the heading "Tell Us Your Favorite Use!"

An Entrepreneurial Moment of Truth

For many entrepreneurs, the "big idea" epiphany comes as they watch, observe, and seek to understand (1) the unsolved pain customers are experiencing and (2) the current (clumsy) and new (elegant) solutions customers may use to stop the pain. In a simple model, pain is the barrier. Customers look for ways to get through or around these barriers that cause pain. Smart entrepreneurs view these behaviors to reduce pain as big opportunities for new ideas, i.e., for competitive angles.

In 1985, consumers started purchasing desktop computers from Dell, a new and relatively unknown computer company,

---

[2] *Discovering What Has Already Been Discovered: Why Did Your Customers Hire Your Product?* by Clayton Christensen, Harvard Business School Press.

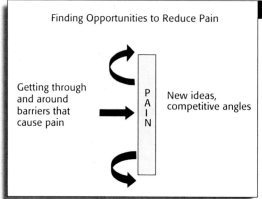

Finding Opportunities to Reduce Pain

Break Through the Pain Barrier

Customers desperately look for ways to go through or get around barriers that cause pain.

Getting through and around barriers that cause pain

PAIN

New ideas, competitive angles

rather than from well-known, established firms such as IBM, Compaq, or Digital Equipment Corporation. Why? Simply put, Dell's direct business model, selling computer systems directly to the customers, reduced pain for consumers by eliminating unnecessary time, costs, and techno-speak sales pitches. The pain for consumers, high prices and non-customized systems with often out-of-date technology, was the result of "brick and mortar" slow-moving retailers with slow-moving merchandise. The direct model allowed Dell to build systems to order, with the latest gee-whiz technology, at competitive prices. This was, and is today, Dell's obvious relative advantage. And the results: reduced pain for consumers and a very profitable business model for Dell. Find the pain, get the gain.

Can You Find Pain in a Dentist's Office?

Where is the pain in the dentist's office? Our first response is, "It's in the dental chair!" We've all been there. We have felt the pain. But if you can, forget about your pain for a moment and ask yourself, where is the pain for the dentist? For our answer, let's think about the dentist's business model. How does a dentist make money? In its simplest form, the dentist's business model is drill, fill, and bill. So, where is the pain? Kimball Wirig, one of the founders of Dentrix Dental Systems, Inc., spent two years in dentists' offices observing, watching, and making notes. He discovered that the pain for dentists is bridging the gap between filling and billing. The dentist performs procedures in the operatory, i.e., the chair, and then sends the patient's file to the front desk for billing. The pain occurs when information about the dental procedure is lost or distorted along the way. For example, the dentist's handwriting may be difficult to decipher, thus causing misinterpretation by front-desk personnel. Overspray from the procedure may smudge the dentist's handwriting, leaving the file illegible. Papers, documents, and charts from the folder may unexpectedly disappear as the file travels from operatory to front desk. Lost or distorted information from the patient's chart means lost revenue. Lost revenue spells pain for the dentist. Kimball Wirig's research led to the development of a usage-specific management system custom-fit for dentists. The Dentrix Dental System is the first management software designed to connect the operatory to the front desk, minimizing information loss and distortion. The result: reduced pain for dentists and extraordinary profits for Dentrix.

Target the Pain

Now let's think about prescription drugs. Where is the unsolved pain for consumers? Certainly the sticker-shock price can cause pain. Side effects may cause pain. What about the packaging? How could the packaging cause pain? Consider the typical brown or white prescription drug container. They all look the same, yet they are all different: label size, label position, number of stickers, text font, information positioning, amount of information, format of instructions. These differences from bottle to bottle and from pharmacy to pharmacy can cause confusion, and confusion can cause medication errors. Of course, medication errors and even the anxiety over the possibility of making such errors can cause pain.

Deborah Adler, a graphic designer, provided the prescription for this confusion and pain. She was inspired to develop a new container system after her grandmother accidentally swallowed pills meant for her grandfather. She is not alone. Research conducted by Target suggests that 60% of prescription-drug users have taken medication incorrectly.

Alder and industrial designer Klaus Rosburg turned the traditional prescription-drug bottle on its head so that the label could be wrapped around the top. Then they flattened the container so patients could read the label without rotating the container. The label is divided, by a horizontal line, into primary and secondary information. The primary or most important information (drug name and dosage) is placed at the top. Six colored rubber rings

that attach to the neck of the bottle enable family members to identify their own medications so prescription drugs in a shared cabinet
will never get mixed up. On the back side are warnings and a pull-
out card with more detailed information. The new prescription-
drug packaging system, adopted by Target, helps prevent mix-ups,
and labels display crucial data, such as drug and dosage, clearly at
the top.

Are You Ice-Screaming for Enjoyment?

Of course, enjoyment and opportunity often produce plenteous
profits. Our fellow creatures appear to be born with sophisticated
and highly-tuned enjoyment-seeking, sameness-avoiding radars
that search out products such as luxury leather-seated automobiles,
high-powered home entertainment systems, decadent chocolate
truffles, expensive cologne packaged in exotic bottles, super-premium ice cream, palatial homes overlooking the golf course, vaca-
tion timeshares, and even Master Replicas Force FX Star Wars light-
sabers.

Consider the entrepreneurs Ben Cohen and Jerry Greenfield.
In 1977, they completed a $5 correspondence course in ice-cream
making. A year later, with a $12,000 investment, they opened Ben
& Jerry's Homemade Ice-Cream Scoop Shop in a renovated gas
station in Burlington, Vermont. On April 12, 2000, the company
was acquired by Unilever for $326 million. Why the success? Ben
and Jerry discovered that a segment of consumers were screaming
for super-premium ice cream with low overrun (air), high fat content, and the highest-quality ingredients, and they were willing to
pay a super-premium price for it. So Ben and Jerry set out to
"make, distribute, and sell the finest quality all-natural ice cream
and euphoric concoctions with a continued commitment to incorporating wholesome, natural ingredients."[3] And they made purchasing and consuming super-fun with such flavors as Cherry Gar-
cia, Chunky Monkey, and Phish Food. Of course, a big key to
success for Ben and Jerry was their ability to capitalize on one of
life's simple pleasures—satisfying taste—and another of life's simple pleasures—rewarding ourselves with the best treat we can pos-
sibly afford.

---

[3] Ben & Jerry's Mission Statement

Which Is More Compelling, Pain Avoiding or Opportunity Seeking?

Which is the more powerful entrepreneurial marketing principle, pain avoiding or opportunity seeking? Both are strong motivators. Both have the potential for creating relative advantage. Again we must defer to the experts. Current research in psychology and economics strongly suggests that people are more motivated by pain avoiding than by opportunity seeking.[4] In fact, studies estimate that pain avoiding is about 2.5 times more "motivating" than enjoyment seeking.

Ethnography is a hot area for pain-finding marketing research. It is used by manufacturing giants like Intel as well as startup companies. Ethnographic tools don't require a big budget. They just require a small dose of training and technology combined with a large dose of empathy and imagination. Reiterating the observations of Clayton Christensen, people understand pain and regularly find clumsy workarounds. Ethnographic observation helps us spot the workarounds. Then, if we can bring some technological expertise to bear, we can substitute high-value solutions for awkward customer-originated solutions.

Best Practice: Make the Pitch

Pitch the business relentlessly. Make it short, 60 seconds or less, and filled with passion. Use the pitch to highlight *reason to believe* and end every pitch by asking for something. Think about baseball for a moment—America's pastime. Whose names come to mind when you think of great baseball pitchers? You may think of Walter Johnson or Grover Alexander or Warren Spahn or Sandy Koufax or Bob Gibson or Steve Carlton or Nolan Ryan or Roger Clemens or Randy Johnson or Greg Maddux. If we use total wins as the sole criterion, who is the greatest of them all? If you said Cy Young, you are correct. He won 511 games over his 22-year career, an average of about 23 victories a season! Next on the list is Walter John-

---

[4]"Prospect Theory: An Analysis of Decision Under Risk," by Kahneman and Tversky, in *Econometrica* (1979)

son with 417 wins, almost 100 fewer than Cy Young. In 1956, baseball Commissioner Ford Frick introduced the Cy Young Award to honor the best pitchers in the major leagues. Today, the greatest award a pitcher can receive is the Cy Young Award.

So, how did Cy Young win so many games? Baseball Hall of Fame historian Lee Allen[5] wrote, "There have been faster pitchers but Cy Young's control was so unerring and he was so tireless that he just kept throwing as if he were systematically chopping down a tree." He pitched relentlessly and he was a master of control. He holds records for the most games started, with 815, and the most complete games, with 749. He was always pitching. And so it is with successful entrepreneurs. They are always pitching. To win, you have to pitch. A little-known fact about Cy Young is that he also holds the record for the most losses in a career—316. So, he did not win every game, but he did win more than any other pitcher in Major League Baseball.

Making the pitch is about selling, presenting, and pitching the business relentlessly, and highlighting a strong *reason to believe* in the process. We have observed that successful entrepreneurs are always in pitching mode. They never miss an opportunity to pitch the business. Guy Kawasaki[6] highlights this notion of relentless pitching:

Question: How can you tell if an entrepreneur is pitching?
Answer: His lips are moving.

But it's more than moving lips: it is knowing how to connect with your audience. It is designing the pitch to highlight *reason to believe*. It is timing. It is passion. It is persuasion.

Know Your Audience

Because you are selling the business, the audience may be a potential investor. However, the audience also could be a potential partner, board member, supplier, or employee. For our purposes, we will focus on potential investors.

---

[5] Baseball Historian.com
[6] *The Art of the Start*, by Guy Kawasaki (New York, Penguin Group, 2004)

Baseball pitchers do not throw the same pitches to all batters. Great pitchers tailor their pitches to the particular batter. They do this by knowing the batter. They chart the batter. They know his strengths and weaknesses. They know his tendencies. They know the pitches he likes to hit and the pitches that give him trouble. They know which pitches to throw when they are ahead in the count and which pitches to throw when they are behind in the count. With this highly targeted information, they work with the catcher to customize a unique pitching sequence for the batter.

Similarly, you must know your audience so that you can tailor your pitch. Do the research. Find out what is important to your audience. Find out why your audience is interested in hearing your pitch. How does your audience decide whether or not a product will work or have broad appeal? Google the audience, the investor group, the key players, and the industry. Read the press. Ask your network of contacts, associates, neighbors, and friends. Use your *connectors*, described by Malcolm Gladwell as "people with a special gift for bringing the world together."[7] Learn as much as you can about the audience before the pitch. Then tailor your pitch to the audience.

Prepare the Pitch

For entrepreneurs, the purpose of the pitch is to sell the product *and the business*. Don't get caught up in using the entire pitch to tell how great your product is. Sell the business! To sell the business, your pitch must answer six questions:

1. **What is the need or problem you solve?**
2. **What is your angle?**
3. **Who is your target market?**
4. **What is your revenue model?**
5. **Who is your competition?**
6. **Who is on your team?**

---

[7] *The Tipping Point*, by Malcolm Gladwell (New York, Little, Brown and Company, 2000)

Consider the following framework as you prepare your pitch:

Pitching the Business

QUESTIONS	PITCHES	NOTES
What is the need or problem you solve?	Describe the unsolved pain you minimize or the opportunity you create.	When consumers buy a new product, they take a risk. New products must have an obvious relative advantage to overcome risk. Consumers see relative advantage when a product alleviates pain and/or creates opportunity. Extant research suggests that **alleviating pain** is the most powerful element in creating relative advantage.
What is your angle?	Use the five factors of the angle to highlight how your solution is better than current offerings.	What is your solution? How will you differentiate? Your product/service offering must stand for something different that is important to customers.
Who are your target customers?	Describe who will buy your product/service.	Profile the customer groups you will target. What is the market size?
What is your revenue model?	Tell how you expect to make money.	Demonstrate that you can make money with this venture using testimonials, similar business models, and current customers.
Who is your competition?	Describe who will compete for your customers.	Don't have any? Think again. Unless you have a monopoly situation, you have in-kind, or functional competitors.
Who is on your team?	Tell about your team's background and achievements. If you have a strong advisory board, tell the investors who they are and what they have accomplished.	Investors bet on the jockey, not on the horse.

Think Concise, Think Elevator Pitch

In his book *Selling the Invisible*,[8] Harry Beckwith makes a statement that is worth repeating here:

"The more you say, the less people hear."

Pitching the business is not the time to be long-winded. Investors have short attention spans. They hear thousands of pitches, most of them lousy. They want to hear your brief pitch, see your demonstration, make a quick decision about moving forward or not, and then move on. So, start fast. Get to your point quickly. Say less, so investors will hear more. A strong *reason to believe* empowers people to immediately see that the product will work as described.

Think elevator ride. Think about delivering your message in the time span of an elevator ride, say 60 seconds or less. Brevity requires effort and careful planning. Focus your message by providing brief answers to the six questions listed above. Watch a late-night infomercial to see how the experts do it. These advertisers will hit viewers with the same direct message over and over again until viewers either pick up the phone to order or pick up the remote to change the channel.

Your audience may extend the duration of the pitch because you have piqued their interest. They may ask questions, make comments, and provide suggestions. Great! This is what you want. Let the audience engage and lengthen the time. So, think concise, but let the audience's interest drive additional time.

Pitch with Passion and Get Commitment

"Nothing great was ever achieved without enthusiasm."[9]

Investors look beyond the numbers, the market, and the competition. They want to know if you have the drive, motivation, and passion to succeed. Pitch with passion. Show the investors you have the fire in your belly to succeed. You've got to get them enthused about you and your business in a very short period of time.

Bill Joos the Pitch Doctor at Garage Technology Ventures preaches, "A good pitch changes the pulse rate . . . If you can't get

---

[8] *Selling the Invisible*, by Harry Beckwith (New York, Warner Books, 1997)
[9] Ralph Waldo Emerson

me excited about your plan, we're done. You have to change the pulse rate." Change the pulse rate. Pitch with passion. Develop a *reason to believe* that demands attention.

At the end of your pitch, get commitment from the investor to move forward. Ask for something. Ask for investment funds. Ask for a follow-up meeting. Ask the investor to review your business plan. Getting commitment for something helps move toward closure. It also helps you determine where you are in the sales process.

Practice, Practice, Practice

"When you are not practicing, remember, someone somewhere is practicing, and when you meet him he will win."[10]

To win, you have to pitch well. To pitch well, you have to practice and understand how to quickly demonstrate the distinctive benefits of your big idea. Practicing your pitch builds skills and confidence, which leads to effectiveness. There are no shortcuts. You simply have to practice. Guy Kawasaki[11] claims that it takes about 25 times to become familiar and confident with your pitch. So, start practicing. Practice with friends, colleagues, and relatives. Practice in front of the mirror. Videotape your practice. Practice, practice, practice!

Cy Young practiced by throwing anything at everything. "All us Youngs could throw. I use to kill squirrels with a stone when I was a kid, and my granddad once killed a turkey buzzard on the fly with a rock."[12]

Best Practice: Dominate the Situation

Be a situation dominator and find a situation to dominate, and then blow away customer expectations. When we understand the buying situation, we can easily understand needs, wants, and how to deliver superior value. Successful entrepreneurs often turn good

---

[10]Ed Macauley, seven-time NBA All Star and youngest person enshrined in the Basketball Hall of Fame

[11]*The Art of the Start*, by Guy Kawasaki (New York, Penguin Group, 2004)

[12]The Official Web Site of Cy Young, www.cmgworldwide.com

ideas into great ideas by fine-tuning the details to address a specific buying situation. People look for products and make purchases based on situational needs, not according to some demographic profile.

BOOM

THOUGHT 2.3

Consumption situations dictate needs, wants, and how value is delivered. Would you go out for a romantic dinner in the same restaurant where parents take kids for a quick gut fill?

As an example, consider a large automobile manufacturer that wanted to verify the usefulness of a proprietary market segmentation system that relied on demographics such as zip codes, neighborhood characteristics, and household characteristics. The car company sent door-to-door researchers out to very affluent neighborhoods that should have been prime candidates for their upscale automobiles. Researchers looked in garages and driveways. Everyone was surprised at what they found. Rather than garages full of luxury automobiles, researchers found old junkers and economy sedans, as well as small sporty imports. When asked to explain their apparently odd choices, these wealthy consumers said things like, "The junker is for our teenage son; he'll beat it up anyway and we want to save on car insurance," "The Honda is for our daughter in college; she needs something reliable and cheap to run," and "The small sports car is for my wife; I wanted to buy something for her that was going to be fun for the both of us." Needless to say, the automobile manufacturer decided not to subscribe to the proprietary market segmentation system! Now they explore how vehicles compete by buying situation.

The best marketing approaches usually are an outgrowth of understanding who is buying and the situation triggering the need to purchase. In the old days of marketing, the understanding of buyer and situation was captured in a catchphrase, slogan, or jingle, such as the Coca-Cola classic, "It's the Real Thing!" Did recalling that slogan help you recall good experiences with the brand, buyer, and situation? Many people would say yes, yet tackling "situation domination" through using a clever catchphrase or brand name may be too cornball for today's sophisticated consumers. Or is it?

Boudreaux's Butt Paste was developed by a Louisiana pediatrician, "Pappy" Talbot, to treat diaper rash. Dr. George Boudreaux, a local area pharmacist, compounded Butt Paste for customers. In the mid-1990s, Dr. Boudreaux quit his day job to start marketing Butt Paste. He bought an RV and named it the Butt Mobile and traveled around the countryside to trade shows and pharmacies. A regional manager from Wal-Mart was intrigued by the product and conducted an in-store trial. Butt Paste smeared the competition, and since then has been sold by leading mass market retailers such as Wal-Mart and Target.

Butt Paste continues to be a big hit. Just read a sample testimonial: "Boudreaux's Butt Paste is worth its weight in gold. The stuff is really good. Our daughters are in their mid-20s and this product was not available when they were born. However, this has been a staple for my three, now four grandchildren. It is truly a miracle drug. My mother-in-law who is in her 70s uses it for heat rash. It will cure the worst diaper rash overnight!"

Doc Boudreaux's Butt Paste dominates the "sore butt" situation. Athletes like basketball great Shaquille O'Neal, quarterback Peyton Manning, and legendary cyclist Lance Armstrong all swear by the product. Doc has even sponsored a NASCAR racer, Kim Crosby, a former Louisiana school principal, to spread the good news. The audience is right: younger families with babies living in warm climates are very receptive to using the product.

Dominating one situation has led customers to invent their own uses. In addition to treating bottoms, there are reports of the paste being used for acne, chicken pox, shingles, razor burn, poison ivy, fever blisters, and chapped lips. Even farm animals are getting into the Butt Paste game. It is used for soothing the udders of dairy cattle.

Simple Questions That Lead to Situation Domination

To really understand a buying situation, we need to look at it from every possible angle. As an example, let's consider the purchase of prepared meals by businesspeople. The first thing we want to know is which situations trigger the need for businesspeople to purchase prepared meals. There are many possible situations, such as business lunches, working lunches, and dinners for workers putting in some overtime.

We describe these relevant buying situations in the chart below by asking seven questions—a 360-degree review of sorts! Who are the buyers or product users? What are the benefits, both functional and emotional, that buyers are looking for? When is the decision made, i.e., is the purchase planned or on impulse? Where do buyers expect to find the product? Is this a convenience purchase or something that warrants or even benefits from travel to a special destination? Where do buyers go for information about the product, how do they go about making the purchase, and what are any special considerations for easing the purchasing process? What are the key decision drivers for selecting one alternative over another? How do buyers go about consuming or using the product?

A 360 Review of the Buying Situation provides insight and focus to any product idea. It helps us build a deeper understanding of the consumption situation and experience, which, in turn, is the first step in blowing away expectations. As a reminder, lots of huge manufacturers are selling diaper rash ointment and remedies, but no one dominates the situation quite like the runaway champion, Doc Boudreaux's Butt Paste.

360 Review of a Buying Situation

	RELEVANT SITUATION		
QUESTION	BUSINESS LUNCH	WORKING LUNCH	OVERTIME DINNER
Buyers	Clients, Potential New Hires, Retiring Worker or Manager	Busy Managers, Busy Staff	Tired, Busy Workers
Benefits	Reflect Positive Image, Reward, Create Positive Memories	Satisfying, Fast, Fun, Not Messy	Satisfying, Fast, Fun, Inexpensive
Decision Timing	Planned Well in Advance of Event	Often Habitual Purchase, but Can Be Spur of the Moment	Often Habitual Purchase, but Can Be Spur of the Moment
Product Location	May Be Many Miles from Workplace	Within a Few Miles of Workplace	Within a Few Miles of Workplace
Buying Behavior	Ask Employees and Friends for Positive Recommendations, Visit the Restaurant, Expect Something Unique and Special	May Call In an Order, Don't Want to Wait, Send an Intern to Pick Up Meal, May Want a Charge Account	May Call In and Order, Don't Want to Wait, Manager May Pick Up Meal, May Want a Charge Account

360 Review of a Buying Situation (continued)

| | RELEVANT SITUATION | | |
QUESTION	BUSINESS LUNCH	WORKING LUNCH	OVERTIME DINNER
Decision Drivers	Recommendations, Past Experience, Product and Service Quality	Convenience, Satisfying Taste	Convenience, Low Cost
Usage Behavior	Large Gathering, Expect Special Treatment, Don't Want to Wait to Be Served, Don't Want to Be Rushed After Meal	Eat at Desk or in a Conference Room, Usually Dressed for Business	Eat in a Break Room, Usually Casually Dressed

There are many examples of entrepreneurs tapping into the blow-away-expectation power of situation domination. A local sandwich company got its start using the tactic. These hardworking entrepreneurs developed a premium sandwich and promoted it by cutting their sandwiches into bite-sized samples and giving them away to nearby businesses. In addition to getting businesses to try free samples of the product, the entrepreneurs also left coupons behind to promote purchase trial and get the businesses hooked on their tasty meals.

Locating restaurants close to lots of businesses, providing a satisfying yet quick meal, developing a variety of fun products to complement its basic sandwich, and taking the product directly to the business to force trial all were keys to success for the upstart sandwich maker, who now has over 100 franchise stores. All the success factors, by the way, can be identified from the 360 Review of the Buying Situation described above.

Conducting a 360 Review of the Buying Situation is a powerful marketing tool as well as a powerful method for market segmentation. Whatever the product category, improve your understanding of the market by thinking through all of the possible buying situations, and then answering seven simple questions for each situation:

1. Who are the buyers?
2. What are the benefits?
3. When is the purchase decision made?
4. Where do people expect to find the product?
5. How do people go about learning about the product and buying it?
6. Why do people decide to favor one product over another?
7. How is the product used or consumed?

Finally, get at least a rough feel for the sales potential in each situation, and then pick one or more situations to dominate. Win by specializing! Win by being the dominator!

You Don't Know Jack

"Jack of all trades and master of none" is not really a nice way to refer to someone. This backhanded brickbat has been around since at least 1600. It refers to a man from the European Middle Ages who would wander from town to town doing a combination of manual labor and other tinkering, but doing nothing particularly well. We've all heard the phrase, but do we really believe it when starting a business?

Kevin Keller[13] describes Richard Branson as a modern-day "jack of all trades." Richard Branson owns the Virgin brand name. After creating the Virgin record label when he was 21, Branson went on to found Virgin Atlantic Airways, Virgin Vodka, Virgin Cars, Virgin Money, and even Virgin Brides. All in all, Virgin is spread between more than 200 companies, selling a staggeringly diverse set of products including financial services, music stores, beverages, cosmetics, utilities, mobile phones, and every other imaginable online business. In 1999 Virgin earned approximately $5 billion in annual revenues. However, in that same year, only four of its 11 best-known companies made any profit. Keller cites one branding expert who commented, "When I'm delayed on a Virgin train I start wondering about Virgin Atlantic. Every experience of brand counts and negative experiences count even more." Analysts regularly question the prospects of Virgin's long-term financial health.

---

[13] *Strategic Branding Management,* by Kevin Lane Keller

We wonder why Richard Branson is so hung up on naming everything Virgin. We admire his ability to start so many businesses, but why come off as uninspired by calling everything by the same name? Mind share works best when it becomes the focal point for a single product in a single product category sold to a highly specific target audience. Don't sell a generic product with a generic message. For example, don't sell a generic six-foot power cord of generic quality for $4.99 that can be used for everything from entry-level computers to top-of-the-line hi-fi amplifiers. Why not sell a $6,000 six-foot Electra Glide Epiphany X power cord? These six-foot wonders are produced in limited quantity and sold to picky baby boomer audiophiles who wouldn't imagine using anything less than a premium power cord to run their premium electronics. The Electra Glide commands $1,000 per foot pricing, while generic cords bring in less than $1.00 a foot for products that are very nearly functional equivalents. Laser beam focus pays off! Audiophiles say that they can always recognize the premium "wire makers" when they arrive at audio shows. They are the ones with the expensive cars. They know how to make the money.

Stand for Something Different That Is Important

Learning to focus and specialize is more difficult than it seems. But for entrepreneurs, delivering superior value to customers is impossible without it. It is easy to believe you are pointed with the precision of a laser beam when you are really like light bouncing in every direction off a disco ball. When managers try to find a focus for their new product ideas, we tell them to "stand for something," "stand for something different," and "stand for something different that is important."

To cut through the communications callus that characterizes today's media-savvy society, we need to put ourselves out on the razor's edge. Reward doesn't come without risk, and we realize that taking a focus is taking a big risk.

It is imperative that entrepreneurial products "stand for something different." Fortune 500 marketers often grouse over engineering departments that create new and different products that don't meet an "established consumer need." For entrepreneurs, that attitude is worse than a package of month-old baloney. The job of marketing is to make product differences important, i.e., "stand for something different that is important." The job of engineers is to create breakthrough product differences. Blend dissimilar technologies together, find a new application for an old technology, invent a new technology, but do whatever it takes to be different. Without being different and focused on specific usage situations, entrepreneurial products just can't happen.

Best Practice: Earn Credibility, Don't Buy It

Earned media is more powerful than paid media, and as the term suggests, earned media costs a great deal less. Good publicity is an entrepreneur's high bang-for-the-buck alternative to advertising for creating product awareness, building a brand image, and gaining credibility for the business and the product. Publicity is best when it emerges from quantifiable support that highlights product distinctions.

Apple Computer launched the Macintosh computer in 1984 with a splashy Super Bowl ad titled "1984." The ad features a young, athletic woman dressed in orange shorts and a white tank top running through a zombie-like audience of ashen-gray skinheads. Making her way to the front of the comatose knuckleheads, she pauses and then enthusiastically launches a sledgehammer through a Big Blue screen; exploding the boring uniformity and limitations of IBM personal computers and the accompanying rigid, top-down mentality. The voiceover drones ominously, "On January 24th, Apple Computer will introduce Macintosh. And you'll see why 1984 won't be like 1984."

> **BOOM**
> ─THOUGHT 2.4─
> *Media coverage you earn delivers a much bigger "bang for the buck" than media coverage you have to buy. Talk about your product using compelling, newsworthy stories.*

The Macintosh ad launched a computer company and made an impression on the American consciousness that has lasted more than two decades. A great ad, backed up with a product that was measurably and visually quite different than the competition. Entrepreneurs are still enthusiastically launching their own sledgehammers through the blue screens of corporate America.

The Apple ad is so famous that we were surprised when we first found out Apple Computer only paid to show the ad once.

The impact of *earned media* and not *paid media* is what sent "1984" to the top. Repeated free airings of the ad on local and national television stations, augmented by free coverage in magazine and newspaper articles, catapulted its reach and frequency well beyond any single Super Bowl airing.

Since 1984, America keeps watching, but no Super Bowl ad has ever recreated the Apple Macintosh magic, although plenty of advertisers have tried. In those early days of the Super Bowl, no one had given a cutting-edge Hollywood director a huge production budget to craft a mini-film to hawk a new product. The whole story of Apple's "1984" was timely and newsworthy. Going out on a bit of a limb, we don't believe "1984" is necessarily the world's greatest ad ever made, but we do believe it created the greatest media storm around an ad the world has ever seen. The production, airing, and public reaction to the ad combined to make a compelling story the media knew people would want to hear about. That is the secret to earned media: not a splashy ad, but a compelling, newsworthy story that people want to hear about. It wasn't the ad: it was the news behind the ad.

Fame on a Shoestring

Advertising great David Ogilvy was once quoted as saying that positive media coverage (i.e., earned media) is 600% more effective than advertisements (i.e., paid media). That is good news for start-ups operating on a shoestring budget.

© 2009, JupiterImages

Learn to Make Sushi— Only $100

A sushi restaurant decided to sponsor a sushi-making class for the community. The offer caught the attention of local media, who provided tens of thousands of dollars of free television coverage to the restaurant. A television crew promoted the sushi-making class as well as the restaurant directly to the target audience.

Publicity ideas are all around us. Turn on any morning television show and you will see good examples every day of newsworthy products that are quantifiably different than standard fare. Recently, we saw one we liked. An up-and-coming sushi restaurant was featured on a local news program because the chefs were offering a sushi-making class. For $100, aspiring sushi-makers would get four hours of training, a $25 gift certificate toward a meal with a friend, and all the sushi they could make during the class. It was a fun idea that the local media embraced. They sent down a film crew and their "local flavor" newscaster to tell the story. All in all, the restaurant picked up around five minutes of prime media time, an equivalent of tens of thousands of advertising dollars, to promote the class and their sushi directly to their target audience.

What we will call the Oasis Styling Salon offers an even more dramatic example than the sushi restaurant. The story highlights the key to attracting media attention: dreaming up a newsworthy story. For female viewers, what could be more newsworthy than gifting a day at the spa topped off with a stylish hairstyling and cosmetics makeover to a woman recognized in the local community for her years of dedication and service? Well, how about doing all of this on her birthday? Working together with a local television station, the salon identified a worthy recipient, and then had the station's film crew follow every step of the transformation. Her husband was on hand for the reveal, and then escorted her to dinner. With this outstanding and goodhearted idea, the Oasis Styling Salon earned bundles of targeted media coverage, positive publicity, and credibility, not just for offering a terrifically luxurious experience, but for rewarding an outstanding woman.

Give PR a Chance

Over the years, many marketing managers have treated public relations as the poor redheaded stepchild of advertising. It is seen as tactical and not strategic. From an entrepreneur's point of view, that should be a good thing. Getting a startup to hum happens at the tactical level, where the rubber meets the road, and not in the 30,000-foot strategic stratosphere. Still, there are some broad guidelines to consider when putting together an effective publicity campaign. A PR agency we worked with years ago suggested five questions to ask. They strung the five questions into a single sentence. The result ended up as one of those catchy phrases that we just can't get out of our heads. It is, "Who says what to whom, how, and with what effect?"

We've tuned up the questions especially to fit the needs of entrepreneurs: (1) Who is the spokesperson for the product? (2) What is the message that best highlights the product's distinctive reason to believe? (3) Which audiences should we be speaking to? (4) What venue is best to reach our audiences and minimize our budget? (5) What do we want to accomplish (i.e., how will we be advancing the sale or what do we want the audiences to do after seeing the publicity)?

Oddly enough, when putting together a publicity campaign, we need to start by answering the last question first. Knowing what we want to accomplish, i.e., what we want the audience to do, profoundly influences our answers to each of the other four questions. To win at the PR game, entrepreneurs must begin with the end in mind.

There are many sad examples of rookie marketers altogether ignoring the "what do we want to accomplish" question. Several years ago during the halftime of the Super Bowl, a regional telephone company ran a 30-second spot that prominently featured their toll-free number during its last five seconds. Company managers paid overtime so that all of their phone operators would be on hand to cover the certain rush of inbound phone calls to inquire about their new lineup of value-added phone services. Even managers were pressed into weekend service. All the plans were made. All the people were in place. The trouble was, the phones did not ring. Well, that is not quite true. The phone operators did get three or four calls, but they had nothing to do with the television spot. They were routine calls about service outages. No one called, because no one knew they were supposed to call. The spot had nothing to do with new value-added services. The voiceover did not ask viewers to call and inquire about anything. Managers just superimposed the toll-free number on a standard strategic image-building ad, aired the spot during the Super Bowl, and expected the magic to happen. Entrepreneurs can't afford to be so naïve. Every piece of publicity must be designed with a single-minded focus on what you want people to do.

Buying Is Not a Singular Event

We all want to make the sale now, but buying is a process, not a singular event. The process has several stages: a need is triggered, information search and gathering, product comparison and selection, product purchase, repurchase, and post-purchase advocacy. Publicity can enhance credibility by reinforcing quantifiable support and distinctiveness at each stage of the process.

Publicity—for example, the media coverage of the sushi-making class—can trigger a need for aspiring sushi makers. Publicity about a new informative website can direct a consumer's information search in the right direction, the direction of your product. Media coverage of a nationwide happy-customer gathering can make every owner more confident in past purchases and a better advocate for future purchases among friends, family, neighbors, and co-workers.

Take Stock of the Stakeholders

Understanding publicity and how to make it pay off with enhanced credibility also starts with understanding the stakeholders. Before launching a Big Idea, we need to ask ourselves some questions to assess how others will see it. Who are the stakeholders? What are their general feelings about the product and how it should be promoted? Where would they rate the publicity idea on a simple 1-to-10 scale?

For example, consider the story of a startup Internet company listing used cars for sale from local dealership inventories. The dealerships are located in a conservative community. The principal investors are similarly conservative. The chief operating officer/marketing director has been recently hired away from a job in the not-so-conservative Northeast. The CEO/marketing director prefers to work independently. This could be a recipe for disaster. What seems appropriate for the CEO may not be appropriate for the stakeholders, i.e., the community, the dealerships, and the investors. With good intentions, but unaware of the PR stakeholder model, the CEO pushed forward with a "Find Lots of Local Cars in Your Undies" campaign. The campaign had

BOOM
THOUGHT 2.5

No entrepreneur is an island. When deciding how to promote the startup or making other spending decisions, remember there are a lot of stakeholders sitting at the table ready to pass judgment.

some slightly suggestive radio ads, but the highlight was tens of thousands of T-shirts purchased to hand out in the community to generate awareness and positive buzz. "Find lots of local cars in your undies" was printed on the backs of the T-shirts. Within hours of the campaign's kickoff, the principal investor was calling the small startup's chairman of the board. It was late at night when the call came through. The investor was upset. He was getting concerned phone calls from the local community. His own daughter had been teased when wearing one of the "undies" t-shirts by a group of unsavory young men. He wanted the campaign stopped and now.

The CEO had spent $50,000 on the campaign: the entire marketing budget. The radio ads were stopped. Plans to drum up local media coverage and publicity for the campaign were abandoned. The remaining T-shirts were quietly given away at a local raceway on a Sunday afternoon. The "undies" slogan didn't bother the free-spirited raceway patrons. In the end, with no marketing budget and no confidence from the investors, the startup failed. However, we understand that the "undies" T-shirts still go for big bucks on eBay, when you can find one!

Publicity Campaign: "Find Lots of Local Cars in Your Undies"

STAKEHOLDERS	GENERAL FEELINGS	1–10 RATING
Members of Community	Attitudes in the community are somewhat mixed, but many feel that advertisers are evil and conspiring men. Using undies to promote a product is salacious. The Internet is a dangerous place and "undies" sends the wrong message.	5
Local Car Dealerships	Funny idea that will grab attention. The largest dealerships go to great lengths to stay well within the boundaries of the conservative community standards. Bound to have some concerns about how the community will react to "undies."	5
Principal Investors	What will the community think? Our standing in the community could be negatively affected. I don't want to live with an "undies" label for the next decade.	1

Earned media and community buzz highlighting memorable product distinctions are much more effective than advertising when establishing credibility for the product and the business. That is the good news. The bad news is that the entrepreneur must work hard and plan carefully to ensure that earned media and community buzz will be positive. Entrepreneurs work on a small budget and always seem to be tottering between success and failure. Unfortunately, they must walk the line between doing something that will grab a lot of positive public attention and something that will cause public concern and destroy the confidence of investors.

Startups cannot afford to make publicity missteps. Before committing yourself to a Big Idea, spend some time to answer three simple questions. Who are the stakeholders? What are their general feelings about the product and how it should be promoted? How would they rate the publicity idea on a simple 1-to-10 scale?

Best Practice: Hit the Sweet Spot

Be first to create a new category. Don't compete with the big boys: find the sweet spot, and uncover ways to be unique in a way that truly matters to people! Marketing is primarily a battle of concepts, not products and services, where simple ideas beat complex ones and human emotion often trumps simple logic.

BOOM
THOUGHT 2.6

Learn from tennis great John McEnroe. He says that when the sweet spot is larger, the game gets much easier!

John McEnroe may be the greatest tennis player to ever step on the court. As a player, he always was angry. As a retired player, he is still angry. He is angry about the sweet spot. John has two things to say about the sweet spot. First, unless a player consistently uses the sweet spot of the racket, he or she will hit the tennis ball inconsistently around the court. Finding and then using the sweet spot are the keys to winning. Second, he believes that the size of the sweet spot on modern tennis rackets is much too large. It makes the game too easy!

Claim a sweet spot by finding a truly unique area of opportunity for a business venture and then making the area of opportunity as large as possible. Unlike John McEnroe, we want to make the game as easy as we can! Unfortunately, many businesspeople apparently want to make the game difficult. W. Chan Kim and Renee Mauborgne report from a study of 108 companies[14] that 86% of new ventures were simple line extensions—that is, only marginal improvements on existing products. They further report that the line extensions accounted for 62% of revenues, but only 39% of total profits. In contrast, the 14% of new ventures aimed at developing new markets and products earned a whopping 61% of total profits! Evidently, finding and using the sweet spot makes for good business as well as good tennis.

Red Ocean vs. Blue Ocean

Kim and Mauborgne start us down the road to finding a sweet spot by contrasting Red Ocean with Blue Ocean strategy. If you choose to compete in existing market spaces against strong competitors and fight to get a piece of the current customer pie, then you've adopted a Red Ocean strategy. We fear for you, your investors, and your family. Our hands are starting to sweat just thinking about it.

To compete in the warm and friendly Blue Ocean, you must make competitors irrelevant by *creating* an uncontested market space. You must create your own customer pie, not just fight for a piece of it. As the chart below suggests, there are four ways to make money. Make the "easy money" by baking up your own unique and tasty customer pie. Creating an uncontested market space and

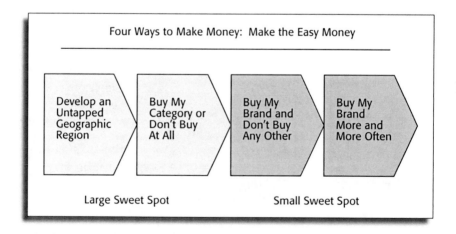

Four Ways to Make Money: Make the Easy Money

Develop an Untapped Geographic Region | Buy My Category or Don't Buy At All | Buy My Brand and Don't Buy Any Other | Buy My Brand More and More Often

Large Sweet Spot   Small Sweet Spot

---

[14]"Blue Ocean Strategy," in *Harvard Business Review* (October 2004)

making easy money, however, requires that you excel in finding un-solved pain, demonstrating unique benefits, exceeding expectations by focusing on specific usage situations, and gaining credibility for the product and the business by highlighting quantifiable support for product claims. Simply adding another brand to a congested market space or dreaming up new usage occasions to increase con-sumption frequency is not enough to earn your place in the Blue Ocean. Your greatest chances for success often come from develop-ing a new category of product or service and/or understanding a region-specific culture well enough to tap into an underdeveloped market opportunity.

Find the Sweet Spot by Avoiding "Me Too" Marketing

To find the sweet spot, we want to find a market space where there are few if any competitors. Create a new category in which to com-pete. The research of Kim and Mauborgne points out, and our own personal experience confirms, that free market space does not come about by technological innovation alone, but by linking new and existing technology to a new competitive angle. To help us explain what we mean by this statement, we must introduce three corollar-ies to Hitting the Sweet Spot. These are "never me too," "play to strength," and "connect product to person."

To begin describing the three corollaries, let's talk a bit about traditional marketing practices. Back in the day when we attended MBA classes, we learned that marketing embodies among the no-blest of human virtues, which is to identify what people want most and create appropriately priced products to fulfill those wants. As faithful followers of *marketing oblige*, we believed that we should interview people about their wants and then bend the will of cor-porate R&D and manufacturing departments to respond to the voice of the people. Sounds reasonable and perhaps even noble, but such thinking promotes investing in line extensions rather than developing new markets and products. **Kim and Mahborgne have already shown how poor that strategy is!** It is the Hollywood equivalent of bad remakes and flat sequels. When asked about films they'd like to have made, it is easy for the movie-going public to say that they'd like to see *Rocky X* or maybe a *King Kong* remake using today's fantastic CGI graphics, but could many of us really imagine a truly great and imaginative film covering new territory or addressing a new market space? As a popular ad campaign tells us, "life comes at you fast," and under that sort of day-to-day pressure we have a hard time seeing past marginal improvements to grasp the truly new and revolutionary. Fact is, people usually define their needs within the narrow confines of what is currently available from familiar brands. Sadly, marketing that asks consumers what they want and then responds to those wants often amounts to nothing more than "me too" marketing. It is *born-to-lose* marketing that chases competitive products and not customer Blue Ocean. It is *please-kick-me* marketing that often puts us in direct conflict with large, well-funded competitors. It is *do-the-impossible* marketing that shrinks the sweet spot rather than enlarging it. It is *go-broke* marketing that makes business success extremely inconsistent and difficult to achieve even for large, well-funded businesses.

"Play to Strength" and Enlarge the Sweet Spot

Some of our favorite manufacturing and technology firms enlarge the sweet spot by carefully observing consumers rather than just interviewing them. For example, consider a manufacturer of farm equipment that placed cameras in the operator cab with farmers to observe how they used it. They were looking for any trouble or workarounds that farmers might have, but perhaps had grown so accustomed to that they wouldn't even think about mentioning them during an interview. Based on the observations, the manufacturer was able to make high-impact changes to the cab layout and controls that significantly improved the usability, and consequently the sales, of their farm equipment.

The general public is not expert in technology or in what is possible with technology. As a result, if we master a technology better than our competitors and have a better grasp on what is possible with the technology, then we have strength. Our strength may or may not already be valued in the market we are targeting. If it is not already valued, all the better; it means we have found a new competitive space . . . a sweet spot. To leverage the sweet spot, we must "play to strength." Playing to strength is a two-step process. First we must master and be known for doing something uniquely well. Then we must link our strength, whether it is technology, know-how, or expert practice, to the buyer's heart.

To reinforce the point, we love to tell the story of the Sony Walkman. Before it was introduced into the market, the Walkman failed to pass muster in consumer research studies. According to marketing researchers, nobody wanted it. Sony pushed on anyway and *played to strength* by leveraging its superior understanding of electronics miniaturization. Deep down, Sony knew that consumers needed the Walkman, even if they said they did not want it. Consequently, the Walkman was designed and manufactured to serve a *latent* need, i.e., a need that is real, but not top-of-mind.

Walkman marketing focused on showing consumers how personalized music solved problems and provided enjoyment they couldn't imagine in their "life comes at you fast world," and the rest is history. Sony linked their superior understanding of a technology to the buyer's heart—their personal space to enjoy their personal tastes.

Leverage the Sweet Spot by "Connecting Product to Person"

Gap analysis is a time-honored fixture that should be in everyone's marketing research toolkit. It is a two-by-two matrix that categorizes product benefits and features along two dimensions: (1) importance to the buyer and (2) performance of the supplier. The general feeling among analysts is that it is best to perform well on

		Sony Walkman Gap Analysis—1978	
	High	Plays Loud Made in USA High-Quality Speakers	
Importance to Buyers			
	Low		Portable Small & Compact Good Headphones
		Low	High
		Performance of Walkman	

product qualities buyers judge to be important. On the other hand, it is acceptable, perhaps even preferred, to perform poorly on product qualities buyers judge to be unimportant. This is good thinking when you are the market leader with "deep pockets." On the other hand, entrepreneurs working from a limited budget following the same approach are likely to suffer death by "me too."

As described earlier, entrepreneurs must look for situations in which they perform best on product qualities that are so new or so unique that most buyers may not even think of them top-of-mind. This is the sweet spot. However, to leverage the sweet spot, an entrepreneur must take the product features they dominate and dramatically increase their perceived importance to the buyer. In other words, they must connect product to person—a key goal of all marketing, but particularly so in entrepreneurial marketing!

Connecting product to person means at least doing a couple of creative things. First, it means making a strong tangible connection between a product benefit and a personal benefit, i.e., the consumer's heart. For example, consider the connection between portable, private music and personal freedom made by marketers of the Sony Walkman. Also, we might want to think over the connection between lightweight, customizable music and the expression of personality made by marketers of the Apple iPod. In addition, connecting product to person means highlighting the product characteristics you own as the supporting foundation for the key product benefits.

For example, Listerine mouthwash tastes bad, much worse than other mouthwashes, so what good is that in a product that people must swish around in their mouths? Well, let's be creative! If something tastes really bad, horrible medicine bad, then it must kill more germs than good-tasting mouthwashes, which in turn makes the mouth fresher and gives people greater confidence when around others.

Who would ever think that "bad taste" would ever translate into market leader? An entrepreneur who understands the Hitting the Sweet Spot would. Listerine has done incredibly well for many years because brand managers found a way to make "bad taste" irresistibly important to mouthwash users. P&G marketers linked a distinctive product feature, that is, "bad taste," to the consumer's heart, that is, "confidence" through the benefit "kills germs." Note that any competitor can claim it "kills germs," but Listerine owns it because it tastes so darn bad.

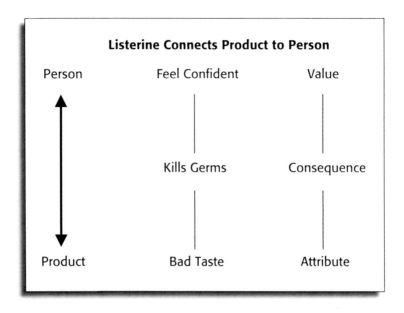

Listerine Connects Product to Person

Person	Feel Confident	Value
	Kills Germs	Consequence
Product	Bad Taste	Attribute

Just Add Sunshine

Del Sol is a terrific entrepreneurial company that is a real hero for finding the sweet spot. They do a tremendous job selling what could be described as very generic products, such as hats, T-shirts, shorts, sunglasses, nail polish, glitter, and other assorted accessories and toys. Every street vendor can offer similar items, except for one important difference. Del Sol products change color when exposed to the UV rays of the sun. That's what we call a great angle. Think how it hits all five factors of the angle litmus test!

Del Sol didn't invent the technology of color change: NASA invented it to use for spacesuit visors. However, Del Sol improved upon the technology and had the creativity to combine it with fun, recreational clothing and accessories. They are the experts in UV color change technology, which enables them to create uniquely colorful and fascinating products that women in particular think are just plain fun to wear. Del Sol avoided "me too" marketing by creating a new category. They "played to strength" by mastering a unique technology (even though it was first developed by someone else). They "connected product to person" by cleverly leveraging the fun factor of their color change know-how through their choice of products (recreational theme), choice of channel (recreational locations), and choice of target (fun-minded men and especially women).

Does finding and using the sweet spot lead to success? In two years, Del Sol went from operating a small cart in a Salt Lake City mall to operating over 100 carts throughout the United States and Canada. Six years later, they were selling products in over 10 countries. Just one year later, they moved out of carts and kiosks to operate 40 retail stores and established direct accounts with Disney and numerous national parks. At their 10-year anniversary, Del Sol set a record for the number of new stores opened in a single year. As the company literature tells us, Del Sol is 100% WOW! Buyers say, "Wow!" when they see their products change into vibrant colors. We say, "Wow!" when we think of how well they have identified and leveraged a sweet spot.

BOOM
THOUGHT 2.7

Inventing a technology is not needed to find a sweet spot. Improving upon an existing technology and applying it in a new way, however, can be pretty sweet!

Review Questions

Define with Five

Define the following vocabulary words using five words or less.

1. Reason to Believe

   _____

2. Unsolved Pain

   _____

3. Earned Media

   _____

4. Play to Strength

   _____

5. Latent Need

   _____

Question the Answer

Answer each phrase below in the form of a question.

1. Who, says what, to whom, how, with what effect.

   _____

2. The ability of a product to reduce pain or create opportunity better than alternatives.

   _____

3. This product asks its customers, "Tell us your favorite use."

---

4. A short, 60-second explanation highlighting a product's benefit and reason to believe.

---

5. Advertising great David Ogilvy said this was 600% more effective than advertisements.

Smarter than an Entrepreneur

Name the product or venture that reinforces or violates a Boom Start best practice.

1. A $300 million marketing budget couldn't get this "pie in the sky" product to fly because its competitive angle was flat and unsharpened.

---

2. A new venture that found pain in the dental office that had nothing to do with bad teeth.

---

3. A new venture that built a successful business around delivering high-quality enjoyment after completing a $5 correspondence course.

---

4. Earned credibility by gifting a day spa and hairstyling makeover to women in the local community renowned for their dedication and service.

---

5. Successfully "played to strength" by leveraging electronics miniaturization even when the results of consumer surveys came back negative.

_____

SuperLaws in Action

Successful products deliver on all five components of Sharpen the Angle.

Activity: Find a product that has (1) strong need to believe, (2) strong reason to believe, (3) blows away expectations, (4) quantifiable support, and (5) makes a unique product claim. Describe how the product meets each of the requirements of Sharpen the Angle.

INSERT A DRAWING
OF THE PRODUCT

Describe how it has a strong need to believe:

Describe how it has a strong reason to believe:

Describe how it blows away expectations:

Describe how it has quantifiable support:

Describe how it makes a unique product claim:

Ride Horses

To get your startup off the ground and increase your speed to market, you need lots of strong backs to help. Pick the best horses you can find and ride them all the way to the bank. After all, no one succeeds entirely on their own.

Horses are people that can help you succeed. In fact, learning to leverage the efforts of others is the *sine qua non* of successful entrepreneurship! Before discussing how to pick horses, let's pause for a moment and make sure you have the right mindset to graduate from Entrepreneurship 101. When you read the following quotes below, do they inspire you? Do they make you want to stand up and shout, "Amen"?

> *"Genius is one percent inspiration, ninety-nine percent perspiration."*
> —Thomas A. Edison

> *"Formula for success: Rise early, work hard, and strike oil."*
> —J. Paul Getty

> *"Life grants nothing to us mortals without hard work."*
> —Horace

Do you believe that working hard is the key to entrepreneurial success? If you do, then you have failed Entrepreneurship 101. That's right! We love hard work as much as the next guy; however, entrepreneurial success is not determined by your hard work, but by the work of significant others, especially powerful horses. The more you leverage the efforts of influential people, the more successful you become. It is not bad to work hard, but it is better to work smart and find horses to ride to the bank. The types of quotes you should be hanging on your wall are as follows:

> *"When a man tells you that he got rich through hard work,
> ask him: Whose?"*
> —Don Marquis

> *"The ladder of success is best climbed by stepping on the rungs
> of opportunity."*
> —Ayn Rand

> *"If I have seen further, it is by standing on the shoulders
> of giants."*
> —Sir Isaac Newton

Instead of working 18 hours every day to grow your business, try standing on the shoulders of powerful horses and look for others to help you succeed. Riding horses is a better way to succeed and a faster way to accelerate the growth of your business. Why walk when you can ride?

Your Champion—Your Horse

In the late 19th century, the quality of a cowboy in the Old American West was directly related to what he rode—his horse or number of horses in the corral. Horses were the main mode of transportation and often used in daily work to plow, clear land, and manage herds. While today, most of us no longer ride horses to generate income, nevertheless they are critical to the success of your startup company.

Horses today are any influencer of your target market. They highlight, defend, and promote your products and/or services to key customers and partners. In short, **they are your champions**. They may be acquaintances, friends, neighbors, board members, association presidents, celebrities, or gurus of your industry. Regardless of their origin, they are *influential people for your target market*; when they speak, potential customers and investors listen. Horses act as your advocates, provide you with hundreds of contacts, and give you instant credibility with key customers and partnerships. A horse can open more doors to your customers in one hour than two years of cold calling on your part. For a new company, it is critical to find local, regional, or national horses. Find your champions and you will find success.

The Value of a Local, Regional, or National Horse

In local markets, you can tap into *local celebrities* and leaders who can help define your product and accelerate the growth of your company. These local horses can be in government or local television, or simply be popular icons in the community. Each has the power to open doors, influence customers, and close deals. In Utah, a popular horse for outdoor merchandise was Doug Miller. Any avid hunter or fisherman was sure to tune in to the show *Outdoors with Doug Miller.* Looking like a big gruff teddy bear, Doug was extremely popular with hunters and fishermen alike. If Doug Miller highlighted your product, it had immediate local awareness and appeal. While Doug's endorsements were not as expensive as those of regional or national horses, Doug was a great horse for local companies getting their outdoor products to market. Using local horses is a good idea when demonstrating *proof of concept* and building initial sales before going regional or national.

BOOM

———THOUGHT 3.1———

In the Old West, the quality of a man was judged by the quality of his horse. The same can be said for the rough-and-tumble world of startup businesses.

Regional or National Horses are, of course, more powerful in reach and impact for your customer base. For more than a decade, there has been no better horse in the world than Oprah Winfrey. Oprah highlights the products and services of women entrepreneurs on her website and is always a cheerleader for the underdog. In 1994, she highlighted the new Enell Sports Bra and the product became an overnight success. After hearing her talk about the product on her show, women throughout the country ran to the stores to purchase new bras.

Want to get your book on the bestseller list? Just convince Oprah to mention it on her show and have it listed on her website under the title "Books Seen on the Show." Oprah Winfrey is a marvel. She is no ordinary horse: she is a unicorn with the magical power to make your product become an overnight success. Find other unicorns in your industry.

How to Feed Your Horse?

Traditional marketing firms know the value of a horse. Firms pay horses millions of dollars to endorse their products or services. The bottom-line impact of having a horse endorse your company can be astounding. With George Foreman as their horse, Salton Corporation sold roughly 40 million grills over the past 10 years. In 1991, Quaker Oats paid Michael Jordan $18 million over a 10-year period to highlight Gatorade. *Fortune* magazine estimates that Nike's selection of Michael Jordan as one of their "horses" has brought Nike over $5.2 billion in revenue for shoes and clothing. That's quite a horse. It is no secret how Fortune 500 companies get horses to endorse their products: they **buy them.** To be perfectly honest, large firms may not even care if horses like or don't like their products. They just pay them to endorse their products. Unfortunately, entrepreneurs don't have that luxury. They can't buy the cooperation and loyalty of horses: they **must earn it**.

BOOM
THOUGHT 3.2

When it comes to horses and endorsers, startups must earn with tons of passion what big companies usually buy with tons of gold.

If you don't have millions of dollars to buy a horse, how can you afford one? There are several ways to attract a horse to your startup company. Many horses are attracted to your company because of recognition, power, credibility, stock options, being on your advisory board, or sometimes just having the opportunity to be associated with a super idea. There is some magical force that pulls horses to you when you have an angle that (1) has the need to believe, (2) has a strong reason to believe, (3) blows away expectations, (4) provides quantifiable support, and (5) has a unique product claim. Horses are attracted to angles like flies are attracted to honey. A horse is a horse of course because they are hip-hop, on the cutting edge, in the know, and like leading the charge. They are just as glad to find you as you are to find them. The key is, you must *search* for them because they don't just show up at your door. With a sharp competitive angle, for a minimum charge or minimal attention, they will help you.

More than 47.5 million LIVESTRONG wristbands have been sold since May of 2004 to raise funds for the Lance Armstrong Foundation. When first asked about the product and his willingness to wear the bracelet, Lance responded, "Someone came up and asked me about wearing one in support of cancer research and I agreed. It seemed like a good idea." Good, strong angles attract powerful horses.

Successful People Ride Horses Too

Who doesn't know Donald Trump, the successful American business executive, author, entrepreneur, and television personality? "The Donald" has written books titled *The Way to the Top: The Best Business Advice* and *Why You Want to Be Rich: Two Men One Message*. His reality show, *The Apprentice*, was a national hit with everyone watching just to hear his famous catchphrase, "You're fired." In Trump's own words, "I mean, there's no arguing. There is no anything. There is no beating around the bush. 'You're fired' is a very strong term."

In 2006, *Forbes* estimated his wealth at $2.94 billion. As a national icon, clearly Donald Trump didn't need a horse, right? No, wrong! Even Donald Trump had a horse, and boy, was it a good one. Trump started his career at his father's company, the Trump Organization. His father, Fred Trump, was not only a mentor, but provided him with millions of dollars to fund his first real estate ventures. It sure pays to have a horse in the family!

Best Practice: Find Benefactors

Early on ask the question, "Who benefits most if I succeed?" Think through the question carefully, because the answer will help you find your initial investors, key strategic partners, and perhaps anchor customers. Learning to ask the *right* questions is fundamental to entrepreneurial success!

If you were in dire straits, who would you turn to for help? Would you try to tap parents, friends, or the local bank? If you were thinking like an entrepreneur, you would look for a benefactor that stands to benefit a lot from your growth and long-term success.

The movie *The Wizard of Oz* is a classic story about finding benefactors. If you remember the story, Dorothy Gale has been caught up in a tornado and carried to the mythical Land of Oz far away from her home in Kansas. Unfortunately for Dorothy, she accidentally kills the Wicked Witch of the East upon her arrival in Oz. Consequently, Dorothy makes quite an enemy out of the Wicked Witch of the West. Nevertheless, Dorothy wants to return to her home in Kansas and decides to travel to the Emerald City to enlist the help of the Great Wizard.

Dorothy knows that she cannot make it to the Emerald City on her own because the Wicked Witch will try to slow her down, stop her, or maybe even kill her. Dorothy needs some benefactors and she keeps an eye open for anyone that will greatly benefit from a trip to the Emerald City. At the journey's outset, Dorothy runs across a scarecrow at a crossroads. She removes a nail to take the scarecrow down from his post and finds out the scarecrow desperately wants a brain. Dorothy suggests that the scarecrow can get a brain from the Wizard in the Emerald City. The scarecrow joins Team Dorothy. Next, the two stumble on a rusted tin man. Dorothy applies the oil can and finds out the tin man desperately wants a heart. Dorothy suggests that the tin man can get a heart from the Wizard in the Emerald City. The tin man is now part of the crew. Not long afterwards, the little group is startled by a lion who attacks the travelers and tries to bite Dorothy's little dog Toto. Dorothy, heedless of the danger, swats the lion on the nose to protect her dog. Dorothy then has to comfort the lion as he whimpers about his nose, and finds out the lion is cowardly and desperately wants courage. Dorothy suggests that the cowardly lion can get courage from the Wizard in the Emerald City. The lion completes the team, and then the three benefactors successfully get Dorothy to the Emerald City.

But the story does not all go in Dorothy's favor. Turns out, the Wizard also needs a few benefactors. He needs someone to kill the Wicked Witch of the West. When Dorothy and her team arrive, the

> # BOOM
> ## THOUGHT 3.3
>
> *Find benefactors by asking yourself who will benefit from your success. Engage benefactors by promising that each will get what they want most if they help make the startup successful.*

Wizard gives everyone the royal treatment. He then gives Team Dorothy an audience and finds out Dorothy desperately wants to return home, the scarecrow desperately wants a brain, the tin man desperately wants a heart, and the lion desperately wants courage. The Wizard promises to give each benefactor what they want most if and when Dorothy brings him the broomstick of the Wicked Witch of the West. The Wizard is very clever. Like Dorothy, he really understands how to spot benefactors. It is an unwritten law of the universe, mysteriously hidden from the majority of humankind, that when you give people what they want, then you get what you want.

Find Benefactors in the Value Chain

Products do not stand alone. Products are part of a value chain that extends from components to customers. Understanding the value chain and where your startup fits in can be a powerful tool to give your new business legs. To find benefactors, explore your product's value chain. Which businesses provide components as inputs to your product? Which businesses use your product as a component for their product? Which retailers sell and service your product or companion products?

DuPont Stainmaster is the world's single bestselling brand of carpet, but not many people know that DuPont doesn't manufacture carpet. DuPont manufactures the nylon and stain-release *sauce* that other manufacturers and carpet mills process to make the carpeting we have in our homes and businesses. DuPont found benefactors to transform the carpet industry from a narrow-margin heartbreaker to a high-flying profit maker. DuPont managers fought commodity nylon prices for generations, but then decided to fight back by offering something that every player in the carpet industry wanted most. Every carpet manufacturer and retailer wanted a premium-priced carpet that consumers would recognize and trust. Everyone in the industry wanted a profitable product that would sell itself. Before Stainmaster, all carpeting looked very much the same to consumers. Since all carpeting looked the same, consumers bought on price—bad news for the entire value chain. Premium-priced, high-quality, easily recognized Stainmaster brand carpet changed all that and consequently found benefactors willing to promote DuPont all along the value chain.

The same principle works in the world of startups. MyFamily is a leading online subscription service for providing genealogical information and collecting family photos. Over the past decade, it has grown rapidly into one of the Internet's top 20 properties. To accelerate their growth, MyFamily raised more than $75 million in funding from benefactors. MyFamily looked at their value chain and asked the question, "Who benefits if I succeed?"

The answers company managers came up with were Intel, Compaq, AOL, and Kodak. Intel benefits because family-history buffs want fast computer processes to digest their mountains of digital photos. Compaq benefits because family-history buffs want new computers with lots of hard drive space, up-to-date memory, and Ethernet connections to access and post online genealogical information. AOL benefits by providing a value-added service to its growing base of family-history buff Internet subscribers. Kodak benefits by repositioning itself in the digital photography sector by building on the traditional strength of family photography. My-Family increases the need for Intel, Compaq, AOL, and Kodak products. In addition to capital raised from these investors, My-Family also received publicity from their association with these companies. At no cost to MyFamily, one national TV spot for Intel prominently featured a shot of the MyFamily webpage.

Banking on a Casino May Not Be a Gamble

If you are down in San Diego, looking to play a little golf, enjoy a monster dinner buffet, sit in on a concert, or spend some time at the gaming tables, you might consider the Sycuan Resort & Casino, operated by the Kumeyaay Nation. The Kumeyaay Nation extends from San Diego and Imperial Counties in California to 60 miles south of the Mexican border.

Realizing that casino customers need easy access to money, San Diego's Borrego Springs Bank approached the Kumeyaay Nation looking for expansion funds. The Native-American-owned bank had come up dry looking for funds through all traditional means, but the Kumeyaay were happy to help. Growing the bank provided Kumeyaay casinos customers with ATMs and a steady supply of cash.

Entrepreneurs can look up the value chain (product source) and down the value chain (product destination) for benefactors. Borrego Springs bankers looked down the value chain to find casinos. The bank provides quick access to money. What kinds of businesses use money like a light bulb uses electricity? A casino is the perfect solution.

All That Glitters Is Not Gold

Entrepreneurs don't discount benefactors that provide support other than funding. Agilix is a software company that specializes in programs for Tablet PCs. In this high-tech product category, Agilix needs capital to fund R&D, but also needs access to programming code and computer hardware technology.

To address the first need, Agilix approached Franklin Covey. Franklin Covey promotes personal planning and saw Agilix as a means to move forward in the electronic planner product space. Agilix got their funding and Franklin Covey got a winning product. Reviewers refer to Agilix-developed TabletPlanner software as marvelous, brilliant, and empowering. Competing with heavyweights like Microsoft, HP, and Corel, TabletPlanner is one of the top 10 best Tablet PC applications.

To address needs beyond R&D capital, Agilix has gone to Microsoft and key computer hardware manufactures. They have become strategic partners that have provided Agilix with access to key technologies, allowing them to be on the cutting edge of this emerging field. As a result of these benefactor alliances, Agilix was able to be one of two software companies to have their software applications ready for the launch of the Windows XP operating system for Tablet PCs. The window of opportunity provided Agilix with market access and a tremendous amount of unpaid publicity.

Best Practice: Prospect for Beta Goldmines

Innovators will not sustain a startup, but they will get it started. Consider mining for gold with the early adopters—customers that will get your startup out of the gate and running!

Many years ago, Pete Seeger wrote the lines, "Oh, had I a golden thread and a needle so fine, I'd weave a magic strand of rainbow design." Every entrepreneur needs to find a golden thread to create a

BOOM
—THOUGHT 3.4—

Beta testers can get startups past the difficult first step of doing business. These early customers are like golden threads leading entrepreneurs to the mother lode!

successful business. Innovation-loving beta-test customers can be that thread.

"Beta test" refers to a stage in the software release life cycle. Software products usually have an alpha stage, that is, a stage in which features are added; a beta stage, in which flaws are removed; and a market-ready stage, in which the product is fully groomed and broadly released to potential buyers.

The beta version is the first version of a product that gets released outside the business. Beta versions help developers evaluate their products in real-world settings. Beta versions are *evaluated* by beta testers. Beta testers can be current or prospective customers. In the software industry, beta testers receive the beta version of a product for free or at a "bargain" price.

When we refer to beta goldmines, we are of course referring to more than just the development of software and to more than just the technical development of a product. Beta testing suggests a process useful for nearly all emerging products and has important marketing as well as technical benefits.

In an entrepreneurial setting, the three biggest challenges with beta testers are to get them (1) to purchase the product, (2) to use the product, and (3) to provide feedback on the product. In our experience, overcoming the first challenge—that is, getting beta testers to purchase the product—goes a long way in solving the other two. Consequently, when looking for beta testers to turn into beta goldmines, picking customers with a strong *need to believe* is a key success factor.

Innovators and Imitators

Markets for new products consist of two types of buyers: innovators and imitators. Research in this area suggests that the number of innovator-buyers can be very small, sometimes as small as 2–3% of the total number of people that will ultimately make purchases in the product category. Nevertheless, these early adopters can get a new idea moving forward and take a startup directly to the mother lode.

Weird Isn't Better

The Dvorak keyboard causes less fatigue and allows faster typing than the traditional QWERTY keyboard. But the Dvorak keyboard is unpopular because it doesn't fit with how we type.

© 2009, JupiterImages

According to the research that has been done to help us understand the diffusion of innovations, three product characteristics stand out as *must-haves* for attracting beta customers. First, the product must have a distinct advantage relative to alternatives. We think of relative advantage in terms of value-in-use. A new product can offer greater value-in-use than alternatives along many different dimensions. For example, compared to existing products, the new product may create greater economic value by being less expensive to purchase, less expensive to operate, less dangerous to use, or less time-consuming to use. Relative to other products, it may also create functional value by being easier or more fun to operate, offering a more complete set of features, or broadening its application to more situations. New products may also create more psychological value than other products by better tapping into emotional needs such as feeling smart, successful, helpful, confident, productive, and so forth.

In addition to superior value-in-use, attractive beta products should also fit with a customer's current way of doing things or daily routine. Consider the Dvorak keyboard. Back in 1936, Dr. Dvorak patented a simplified and *much improved* typewriter keyboard layout to solve the fatigue and inefficiency problems created by the gold-standard QWERTY keyboard layout. In today's world, the use of computers makes the simplified Dvorak keyboard available to anyone who wants it; however, the old QWERTY keyboard introduced back in the 1860s continues to dominate. The Dvorak keyboard fails to please because it does not fit with a customer's current way of doing things.

Usability is another key characteristic. Beta-products suffer when people find them complex to understand or just plain difficult to use. The IBM PCjr of the mid-1980s provides an interesting example. High price and limited software aside, the product was DOA because of its tiny "Chiclet" keyboard, which made typing almost impossible. Evidently, when developing the PCjr, IBM hired usability testers with some mighty dainty fingers.

Beta-test customers become beta goldmines when they become reference points for future customers, provide funding for product R&D, are top prospects for upgraded products, and supply easy access to in-the-field reactions regarding value-in-use, product fit with current practices, and product usability. Beta goldmines are vital for startups. They can provide just enough money and information to keep an entrepreneur limping along on life support until the product and business model come into focus.

Selling the Innovator

Sociologists tell us that innovators are fundamentally different animals than imitators. When it comes to purchasing behavior, innovators (1) want to buy the next new thing before having to pay full price, (2) believe they deserve special consideration because they are taking extra time and effort to test an unproven product, and (3) refuse to sit back and watch anyone else have something new that they don't have.

> # BOOM
> ─────THOUGHT 3.5─────
> *Innovators usually have a different need to believe than do imitators. Successful startups must find a way to sell successfully to both groups.*

Imitators, on the other hand, present their own marketing challenges. Imitators often are apathetic toward anything new and are not shy about expressing their dissatisfaction when something new goes wrong or fails to please.

Sales to innovators can get a new business going. Knowing a little bit about the buying culture of innovators can go a long way in helping entrepreneurs sell to them. First, innovators believe that new technology initially costs more than the old way of doing things, but that costs will come down with time. After all, ENIAC, the first large-scale computer, cost $500,000 back in 1946 and only performed 5,000 operations per second. Today's home computers perform billions of operations per second at less than a hundredth of ENIAC's price tag. Second, innovators apparently can't say no to new technology even when they know it falls way behind on the bang-for-buck power curve. What a dilemma. Innovators crave new technology, but fear they can't afford to buy new technology. Entrepreneurs to the rescue!

Entrepreneurs can attract innovators by asking innovators for their help. By making innovators into product-development partners, startups can offer opportunities for innovators to move quickly and buy new technology at *bargain prices* before it is introduced to the general public at nosebleed *skim-the-cream* prices. But from the perspective of the entrepreneur, offering a *bargain price* does not mean offering a price so low that they won't make any money.

Best Practice: Survive on Rabbits . . . Feast on Elephants

To survive, new businesses must kill rabbits along the way before they kill an elephant. Dream big, but learn to live day-to-day.

Peter Drucker is right: "The purpose of a business is to create and keep a customer."[1] Because customers are willing to pay for products and services, they provide the lifeblood for entrepreneurs—cash! No matter what, don't run out of cash! Nothing else matters if you run out of money. Yet entrepreneurs often overlook ready cash because they are focused on how to get the big customers, the elephant deals. Survival for many new ventures depends on the ability to harvest rabbits along the way. Temporarily getting by with small customers and small earnings is all about survival.

Why Rabbits?

Rabbit-size deals can provide the entrepreneurial venture with life-sustaining cash—money to operate and grow the business—and in-

---
[1] *The Essential Drucker* (2001)

valuable experience. Furthermore, rabbits provide initial feedback and help refine your operations so you will be ready to bring down your first elephant.

Rabbits are easy to hunt, particularly if they run out in the open along your way to bagging the elephant. Rabbits have lower acquisition costs than elephants and lower costs to execute and deliver value. Finding rabbits is not intended to be a long and difficult hunt, but a kill that is made on the way to the elephant. Focus on your contacts, networks, and beta customers. Work every possible relationship that you have to find potential rabbit deals so that little effort, time, and resources have to be spent.

Additionally, the cost of losing a rabbit in terms of company reputation, employee morale, or time investment is significantly less than that of losing an elephant. Shrewd entrepreneurs will see and selectively harvest these rabbits. They learn to survive or live day-to-day on rabbits as they prepare for the elephant deals. We have seen too many startup companies fail because they (1) overlooked rabbits in favor of hunting elephants and subsequently ran out of operating cash, or (2) bagged the elephant first only to learn that they were unprepared to deal with a customer so big, so costly, and so difficult to do business with.

It's the Experience

With rabbits and elephants, it's all about the experience! Rabbits may not provide much money, but they do provide a wealth of experience. The quest for elephants presents a number of unknowns about hunting. What is the landscape? Where are the elephants? How big are they? Are they on the move? What will it take to find and sell to one?

When learning how to hunt, do not begin with elephants. Your equipment may be inadequate and you may lack the experience to bring down such large game. Start small, with something more manageable, like rabbits. Learn to survive on small game first. Then move progressively to larger targets. Get some experience. Practice on rabbits. Learn about the industry, on rabbits. Practice selling, on rabbits. Test new products, on rabbits. The learning, skills, and experience you gain by hunting rabbits will prepare you for the next level—the elephant.

From Rabbits to Riches

In *Forbes*[2] magazine's 2006 ranking of "The World's Billionaires," Sam Walton's heirs held spots 17 through 21 with $15.75 billion each. Combined, their net worth exceeds that of Bill Gates—number one on the list—by $30 billion!

Sam Walton did not start his retail business by feasting on big-city elephants. Just the opposite, he targeted the rabbits of retailing—rural Americans. Although conventional wisdom of the day suggested that a full-line discount store needed a population base of at least 100,000, Walton was not convinced. So he traveled the country studying the discount store concept, exploring geographic markets, and researching competition. He believed that discounting could work in small towns. In 1962, Walton and his brother Bud opened the first Wal-Mart Discount City store in Rogers, Arkansas, after Ben Franklin stores rejected the idea. Walton was convinced that if he "offered prices as good or better than stores in cities that were four hours away by car, people would shop at home."[3] So, he began by locating stores in isolated, rural small towns with populations of 5,000 to 25,000. "Our key strategy was to put good-sized stores into little one-horse towns which everybody else was ignoring."[4] The world's largest retailer started by hunting rabbits. Today, Wal-Mart is the world's leading retailer, with revenues exceeding the GDP of many countries. And it all started when Sam and Bud spotted a rabbit in Rogers, Arkansas.

Take the Scenic Route

When Jim and Sarah Milne decided to combine Sarah's talent for color, texture, and design with Jim's MBA to start Scenic Route Paper Company in 2004, they were thinking big but learned to live day-to-day. Their long-term goal: gain significant shelf space for their scrapbook products with large arts and crafts retailers such as Michael's Crafts, the big elephant. In the short term, however, they were in startup and survival mode. They realized that proven success at the grassroots level would give them the experience, the know-how, and the prowess to hunt the elephant. So, instead of

---

[2] *Forbes* (March 9, 2006)

[3] *Business Week* (November 5, 1979), p. 145

[4] *Sam Walton, Made in America* (New York: Bantam Books, 1992)

racing down the four-lane, busy, competitive highway in search of the elephant, they decided to take the "scenic route" inhabited by rabbits.

For Jim and Sarah, these were small retail outlets, catalogs, and online purchasers. This proved to be a brilliant startup and survival strategy. The cash generated by a few small retailers enabled Scenic Route Paper Company to survive and grow! Today, the company has product distribution in 361 arts and crafts stores, from Magical Memories in Verona Island, Maine to Scrapsession in Beverly Hills, California, and the company has distribution in Australia, Canada, Great Britain, and New Zealand.

Chip Shots and Caveats

Hunting rabbits and elephants comes with five caveats:

1. **If your first kill is an elephant, focus on other elephants**. Some new ventures are fortunate to harvest an elephant right out of the gate. If this is the case for you, then you have proven that you can take down the elephant, make the sale, and deliver the product. Forget rabbits. Start hunting the next elephant.
2. **Watch your resources**. If it takes as much time, resources, and energy to chase rabbits as elephants, go for the elephants. In this case, hunting rabbits wastes valuable resources.
3. **Make the first move**. For certain industries and markets, the first company to make a significant impact gains considerable advantages. This first mover advantage can result in market share, reputation, defining standards, and early profits.[5] Consider a market with relatively few elephants. If you don't get there first, you may not get any at all. Also, consider a market where the first mover is in charge of the rest of the kills. If this is the case for you, forget the rabbits. Move quickly to harvest the first elephant.
4. **Transition from rabbits to elephants**. Along the path to the elephant, you cannot afford to ignore rabbits that will keep you alive and hunting. Rabbits sustain the company until the big revenue is achieved through elephants. When the company starts harvesting elephants, the transition begins. Continuing to hunt rabbits after harvesting elephants is a priority problem.

---

[5] *Competitive Advantage*, Michael Porter (New York: The Free Press, 1985)

5. **If there are no elephants, focus on rabbits**. Some markets don't have elephants. If this is the case, don't ignore the market; elephants may develop. In the meantime, focus on rabbits, with an eye to those rabbits that may turn into elephants.

Best Practice: Weigh Anchor

Anchor customers keep startups going and give it a platform for growing. Finding anchor customers must be a top priority.

For a moment, imagine that different kinds of businesses are like different kinds of ships. The *big business ship* likes to drop anchor in a calm and sunny harbor. The heavy anchor and calm waters make everyone on board the *big business ship* feel safe and secure. The *startup business ship* is like a privateer sailing the open sea. The captain of the *startup business ship* doesn't like to drop anchor. She knows the ship only moves once the anchor is on board. Startup businesses must get an anchor on board before they can start sailing.

Consider the experience of Omniture, a business that helps other businesses understand and manage their Internet marketing channels. Take a look at their customer showcase. There is Toyota, Cadillac, Ford, Microsoft, HP, Oracle, VISA, Ameritrade, ADP, Xerox, Siemens, Tyco, HBO, Fox, CBS, Wal-Mart, Mary Kay, eBay, and the list goes on. Omniture always had great products and talented employees, but their success story really got started with two anchor customers, Microsoft and eBay. According to their CEO, before landing these customers, the Omniture sales cycle was a long and painful nine months. Prospective clients had lots of questions about financial stability, technology, and service quality. With the anchors on board, most of the prospective clients' questions were answered with two words: Microsoft and eBay. The sales cycle shrank to a manageable three months.

> **BOOM**
> THOUGHT 3.6
>
> *Like ships at sea, new businesses don't start sailing until the anchor is pulled on board. Anchors cover costs, help work out kinks in the product and business model, and attract new customers.*

Winning Anchors

Omniture won anchor customers by "promising the world and then delivering." Many in the business questioned whether Omniture would make money with such a policy, but the CEO moved forward anyway. Ultimately, eBay and Microsoft did produce profits, but more importantly produced high-margin, quick-turn-around sales opportunities.

The need for anchor customers is nothing new. For example, a local bakery got its start by providing low-priced, high-quality bread and other baked goods to area restaurants, cafeterias, and catering services. These businesses were their anchor customers. With the anchors established, the bakery built brick-and-mortar retail stores, charged premium prices for their tried-and-true products, and even added a few new products not offered through other marketing channels.

In the manufacturing world, new factories get built by making commodity goods that "fill the factory" with high-volume, low- or no-margin production. Once the factory is rolling, design engineers and marketers start looking for opportunities to swap out the manufacture of low-margin goods with high-margin goods. Not every manufacturer, however, has the good sense to bring anchor customers on board before building a new factory. Based on sales forecasts for 20,000 vehicles per year, General Motors built the Reatta Craft Centre in Lansing, Michigan to produce the Buick Reatta. The Buick Reatta was a state-of-the-art car and the Reatta Craft Centre was a state-of-the-art factory solely dedicated to manufacturing the handmade luxury sport coupe. Managers had high hopes for the car successfully competing head-to-head with European luxury imports BMW, Mercedes, and Porsche. End of the day, the Buick Reatta carried a similar price tag to the European imports, but unfortunately could not match their performance or brand appeal. To make matters worse, the sophisticated electronics used on the Reatta's dashboard did not sit well with Buick's traditional customers. Just over 20,000 total vehicles were sold in the four years before GM closed down the new factory. Millions of dollars and hundreds of jobs were lost. If a company as well-funded as General Motors needs an anchor customer to successfully launch a new product, then entrepreneurs certainly shouldn't try to survive without one.

Anchor customers get your startup going and keep paying the operating bills through good times and bad. No one gets "rich" from what an anchor customer is willing to pay, but these customers will create a foundation from which to grow into profitability.

A Tale of Two Contractors

In the first few years of business, two partners split from each other. One partner formed Boberg Engineering & Contracting. The other partner formed another company that we will call Cottonwood Contracting. Cottonwood eagerly pursued every job opportunity and apparently went by the slogan "If no one else would, Cottonwood." In contrast, Boberg Engineering first concentrated on lining up low-pay, steady work, and then was selective with the bids they put out for any new work.

Boberg would bid on most jobs that invited them, but would bid high on dangerous or undesirable jobs. This way the company could add profitable customers to their anchor customers and not take marginal jobs with small or overly demanding clients that might put the company's future at risk. There came a time when both Boberg Engineering and Cottonwood Contracting were invited to bid on the same risky job. Boberg did not want or need the job now that they had anchor customers providing a steady stream of work. Cottonwood Contracting was still living up to its slogan and bid low against the advice of friends at Boberg Engineering. The job would require large investments in capital to prepare either engineering firm to handle the work load, and the work itself was probably too hazardous for a small company to safely manage. Cottonwood Contracting won the bid, had an employee die on the work site, and afterwards teetered on the verge of bankruptcy. Without anchor customers, Cottonwood Contracting felt pressured to bid low and accept every job that came along, much like a ship being tossed high and low by angry seas.

Hunting an Anchor Customer *

What sort of customer makes a good anchor? The selection is important because potential anchors are customers big enough to set you sailing, but also may be big enough to sink you. Obviously, an anchor needs to be a major player with great brand recognition and a reputation for quality. An anchor needs to be visible and be willing to help make your product visible. Just mentioning the anchor's name to a prospective customer should create feelings of interest and credibility.

Perhaps the biggest decision point is whether the potential anchor is more likely to foster a startup business or let it flounder. Unfortunately, we have seen far too many examples of the latter rather than the former. Startups the size of a dinghy go down fast when they take on an anchor fit for an ocean liner. Every time an entrepreneur walks through our office door to announce they've landed a big account with a national retailer such as Costco, Wal-Mart, or Home Depot, we get nervous. Don't get us wrong—these are wonderful companies that provide tremendous value for customers. However, these companies simply are not geared up to foster most startups. For example, one new business signed a contract with a national retailer but missed the deadline for delivering their product to the appointed distribution center by several hours. The national retailer declined to reschedule a pickup and told the new business to wait another year before trying again. Yet another new business shipped inventory worth hundreds of thousands of dollars to a national retailer notorious for paying vendors slowly. The entrepreneurs, having taken out second mortgages and maxed out credit cards, got nervous and tried to pressure the retailer into paying with aggressive, bordering on rude and unprofessional phone calls and letters. In response, the retailer returned the entire inventory. The entrepreneurs were then left with lots of debt, lots of inventory, and few prospects for earning any revenue.

Attracting and Retaining Anchors with Faster, Better, Cheaper

Potential anchors and the marketplace often measure the merit of new products using three criteria: faster, better, cheaper. These three criteria are the lowest common denominators of entrepreneurship. According to researchers, of all the factors that influence the diffusion of innovation, relative advantage has the greatest impact. Faster, better, cheaper are advantages we know potential anchors and prospective buyers want without having to ask.

Faster, better, cheaper—you either love the phrase or hate it. Consumers love it. Design engineers hate it. Perspectives change based on whether you are the buyer or the maker. Designers know that when they are forced to make something faster and cheaper, it definitely is not going to be better. Even consumers feel the risk when faced with a decision to switch from their premium-priced favorite brand to a bargain-priced unknown brand. That is why branded aspirin outsells the generic two-to-one, even though the generic costs half as much. John Ruskin, the 19th-century English thinker and author, expresses the concern shared by many of us:

> *There is nothing in the world that some man cannot make a little worse and sell a little cheaper, and he who considers price only is that man's lawful prey.*

To help entrepreneurs hit the "sweet spot" with anchor customers, we need to define how much faster, how much cheaper, and how much better a product must be before it has a good chance to overcome the physical, financial, and emotional risks people face when making purchasing decisions.

In Search of Excellence author Tom Peters describes how much faster in these terms. "Insurance claims that require only 17 minutes of actual work yet have a cycle time of 23 days to finalize are outrageous." "Take something that requires others months to do and do it in seconds." Obviously, Tom Peters is not talking about small, incremental changes. Hyperbole aside, delivering "shocking levels" of speed and responsiveness creates satisfying consumption experiences that overcome the doubts of new adopters and reassure anchor customers. From years of doing research in the customer service industry, whether it be selling hamburgers or servicing computers, customer satisfaction hinges on perceptions of courtesy and competency. And to a large part, speed is the biggest driver of both. Incrementally faster is not enough to attract attention. When selling faster, don't settle for anything less than revolutionary.

Faster appears to be universally appreciated. Not so for "better." Better is a funny quality. What is better for one person may be worse for another. Even the old maxim from economics class, "more is better than less," is frequently violated by real-world decision makers. We often think of "better" in terms of ideal points, and ideal points are like opinions: everyone has one. Name nearly any characteristic—sweetness, sourness, heft, detail, brightness, size, or softness—and everyone is in search of not too much, not too little, but just right. Every customer group is a Goldilocks of sorts. To hit the ideal point, entrepreneurs must hone the product concept to fit exactly with the special needs of the person and situation.

Achieving "better" requires entrepreneurs to dominate a situation. As faster must be much faster to gain product champions, better must be much better, and that usually happens in the context of solving a specific problem for a specific set of people.

Of faster, better, and cheaper, cheaper may be the most difficult concept to master. In his research into the impact of cheaper on consumers,[6] Richard Thaler discovered that a much higher percentage of people would drive across town to save $5 on a $15 item than would drive the same distance to save $5 on a $1500 item. Odd, isn't it? Apparently a $5 savings has a different value depending on the discount percentage it represents.

> ## BOOM
> ### THOUGHT 3.7
> *Faster, better, cheaper is a great concept, but keep in mind that* better *must be defined through the eyes of customers who often view features as* ideal points *rather than* more is better.

Cheaper evidently is measured in terms of percent savings relative to some reference price. The entrepreneur can provide the reference price, or it may be a price the potential customer has learned from personal experience buying products in the product category. Obviously, up to a point, the higher the reference price, the better. On the other hand, price often signals quality. It is only reasonable to assume that if the discount off the reference price is too large, let's say 50% or more, potential customers may start having doubts about quality.

Playing the "cheap card" is like walking a tightrope. The product must be cheap enough, relative to a reference price, to overcome the feelings of risk that people naturally associate with trying a new product or brand, but not so low as to create worries about buying a poor-quality product. To quantify the right degree of cheap, we often use the Van Westendorp Price Sensitivity Meter, named for Dutch economist Peter H. Van Westendorp. We won't go into a lot of detail other than to list the four questions we ask to calibrate the meter and to say that we like to provide a range of prices for consumers to react to.

1. At what price do you begin to feel the product is *getting too expensive* for you to consider purchasing it?

---

[6] "Mental Accounting and Consumer Choice," by Richard Thaler, in *Marketing Science* (1985), Vol. 4, 199–214

2. At what price do you begin to feel the product is *getting too inexpensive* for you to trust the quality of the product?
3. At what price do you begin to feel the product is *starting to get expensive*, so that you would start having second thoughts about purchasing it?
4. At what price do you feel that you would be getting a *great buy for the money?*

In question four, we ask for the "cheap" price that represents a bargain, but one that is higher than the "too cheap" price we determine with question two. Van Westendorp Price Sensitivity Research is not the most sophisticated pricing model available, but it does provide very reasonable guidelines for the percent discount required to attract rather than scare away customers.

Anchor Customers Rarely Trade Off Quality for Cheaper

To be effective, cheaper must be much cheaper without sacrificing quality. Not an easy task, but one that often works best when entrepreneurs compete with function rather than head-to-head against products of a similar kind. Anchor customers are looking for technology breakthroughs that, once mature, will provide as good or better functionality at prices substantially lower than those of old technology products.

There are a lot of examples of functional competitors taking down industries of complacent in-kind competitors. With the commercialization of the compact disc and compact disc players, Sony and Philips undercut and eliminated major competitors manufacturing analog audio equipment such as record players and tape recorders. Why try to make a cheaper, yet better record player or tape recorder? Why not eliminate a whole industry with a superior technology that delivers high-fidelity sound with a low-fidelity price tag? Technology trumps brand equity and habitual buying. Digital photography is quickly eliminating film photography because the new technology delivers a much lower operating cost and the instant gratification of immediately seeing your photos. The Internet is replacing newspapers and magazines because of its lower cost and immediacy. Wal-Mart rules because it reduces everyone's cost of living and conveniently brings together, into one location, a warehouse full of everyday products and foods. Examples are even more numerous in business-to-business markets, in which entrepreneurs have brought to bear new technologies to lower costs and displace old technologies and old industries: nylon replaces silk; Tyvek replaces satin; plastic replaces steel; flash memory replaces computer hard drives; and on and on.

Best Practice: Make Heroes

Running a startup is like running a marathon. After inviting all your employees, key customers, and strategic partners to join you in the race, there are two ways to run it. The first way is to run the 26.2 miles as fast as you can and show your partners and cheering crowds that you are far superior to everyone by crossing the finish line first. Clearly everyone will be amazed at your strength, speed, and endurance. All of the glory will be heaped on you!

Successful entrepreneurs, however, have learned a better way to run a marathon. Even though they suspect they are faster and stronger than everyone else, they run at the same pace as their employees, customers, and strategic partners. They use their extra strength to cheer everyone on through the entire 26.2-mile race. At the end of the run, they make sure they are the last to cross the finish line. Why? Because successful entrepreneurs have learned to find ways to make their suppliers, partners, employees, and customers into heroes, because the successful entrepreneur knows that no one can make it on their own. There is plenty of time for the entrepreneur to be a hero ... after the money is in the bank!

It's human nature to attribute success to ourselves. Conversely, we tend to attribute failure to somebody else or to something else. For example, when we get a new client, when we increase revenues, or when we reach our profitability goals, we attribute these successes to our business smarts, to our unique product ideas, or to our outstanding company. If our performance turns south, however, we tend to look elsewhere for reasons to explain such poor performance: the poor supplier, the bad weather, the soft economy, the powerful competition. These explanations of success or failure fit nicely into classic *Attribution Theory*. Simply stated, we have a strong need to understand and explain the world around us and attribute all the bad stuff to anyone other than ourselves! This is particularly true for us entrepreneurs. We attempt to explain why we succeed or fail by using internal or external attributions. When we use internal attributions, we claim that we are directly responsible for the outcome. We are the heroes. And of course, when we use external attributions, we assign responsibility for the outcome to an outside agent, such as a supplier, a partner, a competitor . . . or an outside force, such as the economy, the weather, or the stars.

Since we rely on significant others for our success, we must find ways to make heroes out of our suppliers, partners, employees, and customers. Successful entrepreneurs deflect the spotlight from themselves and attribute success to those who help them reach it. Generating heroes will do much more to build sales and profits than generating self-promoting press releases.

Where to Start?

In the early days of Dentrix, the dental practice management system, the founders faced a critical decision: "How do we reach the target market—dentists?" They had two choices: (1) develop a company sales force or (2) outsource the selling function to independent sales agents such as distributors or value-added resellers, i.e., VARs. Given the complex and technical nature of the product and given that the founders wanted control over the selling function, their preference was to develop a company sales force. When they considered the costs of developing a company sales force, however, they quickly opted to use distributors. Simply put, they could not afford to build their own sales force, so they focused on finding and developing distributors to do the selling for them. This proved to be a smart decision, because they found distributors who already had strong business relationships with dentists. The distributors used these relationships to introduce the Dentrix products. Because of the established trust, dentists were willing to consider and even try this new product. Also, Dentrix paid these distributors on commission and only when a system sold. Of course, this helped the company's cash flow situation, but that was not all. Dentrix made these distributors heroes. They provided quality products, on-time delivery, and customer telephone support. As a result, these distributors became heroes in the eyes of the dentists, because they provided solutions to salient practice management problems. And these distributors became very wealthy.

Don't Forget Your Own Front Line

Consider the power of your front-line employees. These are the people in your company who have the one-to-one business relationship with your customers. These people are the face of your business. Of course, with a new venture, you may be the front-line employee, or you may only have one or two front-line employees. John W. Nordstrom and Leon Leonwood (L. L.) Bean, two entrepreneurs from the retailing sector, found great success by making heroes out of their sales associates. In their book, *The Nordstrom Way*, Robert Spector and Patrick McCarthy point out that "Nordstrom expects, encourages, preaches, and demands individual initiative from the people who are on the front lines ...The best Nordstrom sales associates will do virtually everything they can to make sure a shopper leaves the store a satisfied customer."[7] And one of the keys to Nordstrom's success: "Motivated employees perform 'heroics,' i.e., acts of outstanding customer service, which are part of the Nordstrom mystique."[8] The stories about heroic acts of customer service at Nordstrom are almost endless. Associates have been known to hand-deliver special orders to customers at their homes and even find merchandise at other retailers for their customers. Handwritten thank-you cards are common, along with telephone calls and emails. Customers who return products to Nordstrom are not subjected to an inquisition, but are treated with respect and courtesy as the heroic sales associate comes to their aid with exchange suggestions or cash refunds. We agree with Tom Peters, "Nobody does it better than Nordstrom."

In 1911, Leon Leonwood Bean created the Maine Hunting Shoe, a lightweight, waterproof shoe with rubber bottoms and leather uppers. With each pair of shoes, Bean included the following note:

> *I do not consider a sale complete until goods are worn out and customer still satisfied.*

Although 90 of the first 100 boots were defective, because the rubber bottoms separated from the leather uppers, Bean delivered on his promise and repaired the boots or refunded the money. This almost put him out of business, but he kept his promise. The rest

---

[7] *The Nordstrom Way*, by Robert Spector and Patrick D. McCarthy (New York: Wiley, 1995)
[8] Ibid.

of the story is that Bean perfected the boot and delivered customer satisfaction. The company that created the Maine Hunting Shoe became an American entrepreneurial success story. Bean's golden rule remains in the company today:

Sell good merchandise at a reasonable profit, treat your customers like human beings and they'll always come back for more.

And who, more than anyone in the organization, has the ability to implement Bean's golden rule? These are the front-line employees.

A few years ago, we toured the L. L. Bean store and offices in Freeport, Maine. We wanted to learn firsthand about the company's legendary front-line associates. As we walked through the facility, we noticed a credo prominently displayed in many of the offices:

A customer is the most important person in our organization— in person or by mail.

A customer is not dependent on us. We are dependent on him.

A customer is not an interruption to our work. He is the purpose of it.

We are not doing him a favor by serving him. He is doing us a favor by giving us the opportunity to do so.

Not content to simply read the credo, we asked employees and sales associates about this customer service philosophy. Without an exception, the responses were, "We live by this!" And it shows.

So, make your front-line employees heroes. Enable them to perform heroic acts for customers. Provide them with the necessary products, tools, and support to make them successful. Then, heap recognition on them. Attribute your success to them. You'll find that generating heroes among the front-line employees will generate sales and profits for your company.

Make Your Customers the Heroes

You might remember the Home Depot ad campaign highlighting Dad as the hero. In the first few frames of the TV advertisement, a young boy tells his friends that he and his dad are going to build a tree house. At the same time and in a different location, the dad is telling the Home Depot associate that he has no clue about which materials to buy, which tools to use, or just how to go about building a tree house. Of course, a key message of the ad comes next when the Home Depot associate helps the dad figure it all out. Then we hear the tag line "You can do it. We can help."

The closing frames show the hero dad with his young son, enjoying the tree house they built together. And the important learning point? Home Depot is not claiming hero status. Dad is the hero. Home Depot makes Dad the hero. When you make your customers the heroes, they will come back for more.

Best Practice: Unleash the Love Group

Call them what you like—loyal customers, brand champions, or the Love Group—we can't say enough about how important they are to growing a startup business. Think of them as a huge herd of wild stallions that will respond to your command and set the tone for everyone that sees them. Discover what your customers love and take their message to the undecided and uninformed. Don't use time and energy to fight cynics and hecklers. Learn to focus on the love and take your product to unexpected heights.

> **BOOM**
> ──THOUGHT **3.8**──
>
> *Find your* Love Group, *i.e., brand champions, and never let go. Far too many managers have turned their backs on their* Love Groups *and lost their businesses.*

There are a lot of ways to divide up or "segment" a market into manageable chunks. If you've read the mainstream marketing textbooks, you'll probably remember the usual dividing lines separating groups of people: things like demographics, psychographics, lifestyles, benefits sought, product usage, etc. Our favorite segmentation approach, however, is borrowed from politics. Political strategists and candidates look at the world and their task in very simple terms. Voters are separated into three groups: Pro, Swing, and Anti. Just to make things a little more interesting, we refer to the groups as Love, Swing, and Hate.

The task during an election year is to retain the Love Group and capture enough of the Swing Group to get elected. It is a difficult juggling act. Candidates need to earn at least 50% of the vote, but can't slide by telling people only what they want to hear. In today's media environment, flip-flop candidates can't succeed when delivering one message to one group and a conflicting message to another group. Candidates need a consistent message that rings true with the Love Group while at the same time finding ways to help the Swing Group see the issues through the eyes of the Love Group. Success or failure hinges on a candidate's ability to engage and tap into the power of core voters—that is, the Love Group.

Oddly enough, the truth of Love Group political reality is often lost on modern-day marketers. Companies walk away from and turn their backs on their Love Groups all the time in search of new sets of customers that, more times than not, flat-out refuse their tender advances. "This is not your father's Oldsmobile," the infamous GM tagline aimed at rejuvenating the brand, must have confused and perhaps even embarrassed Oldsmobile loyalists. "If this isn't my father's Oldsmobile, the car that signals middle-class success without the class-conscious conceit of a Cadillac, then what is it?" And the flashy multi-million-dollar ad campaigns didn't win a new Love Group featuring Star Trek Captain William Shatner and his daughter, even when the tagline was later changed to "We have got a brand new Oldsmobile, this is a new generation of Olds." The Oldsmobile was phased out and buried in 2004. GM marketers walked away from the Love Group and managed to kill the oldest automobile brand in the world. Since 1897, the Oldsmobile had survived through all the bad times, the war times, and the foreign car invasion times, but couldn't survive the MBA (murder brand assets) treatment.

Announcing, "This is not your father's Oldsmobile," was like saying, "This is not your father's Coca-Cola." Who would ever think of messing with the number-one brand in the world with a record for success dating back to 1884? Oh wait, Classic Coke *was* pulled from the market in 1985 to make way for the more hip and sweeter-tasting New Coke. Executives were concerned that Classic Coke wasn't faring well in blind taste tests against archrival Pepsi-Cola. Coke formulators were sent to work formulating, and New Coke was born. It won the taste tests. It was noticeably sweeter than the old Coca-Cola. In fact, it tasted more like Pepsi than Coke. New Coke was heralded with an enormous marketing campaign. Executives scoffed when warned by consultants to not walk away from the Love Group by pulling the old in favor of the new.

Executive confidence increased when New Coke sales spiked promisingly for several weeks, and then 100 years of history and an angry Love Group fought back. Public outrage spearheaded by the organization Old Cola Drinkers of America forced Coca-Cola to reintroduce Classic Coke less than three months after the introduction of New Coke with the simple statement from company director Donald Keough, "The simple fact is that all the time and money and skill poured into consumer research on the new Coca-Cola could not measure or reveal the deep and abiding emotional attachment to original Coca-Cola felt by so many people."

Know Thy Love Group

We frequently ask aspiring entrepreneurs, "Who is in your Love Group?" We rarely get back a focused and definitive answer. The fact is that most startups can't identify who faithfully purchases their products beyond offering up a few demographics like average age, gender split, and regional sales percentages.

Entrepreneurs can't afford to be that cavalier. The Love Group is their lifeblood. Just like a political candidate, entrepreneurs must know and retain their Love Group while at the same time helping the fence-sitters see their product through the eyes of the Love Group. Entrepreneurs don't need 50% of the popular vote to succeed, but do need a strong core audience that they thoroughly understand. By thoroughly understand, we are talking about drawing together a customer profile that looks more like an ethnographic Mona Lisa than a demographic stick figure. What do customers look like, how do they express themselves, what do they read and watch, where do they live, what vehicles do they drive, what are their hopes and aspirations, and most important, which of our product features and benefits really get them going?

Several years ago, the plastics industry was struggling with growing public concerns over recycling and resource use. Special interest groups were successfully encouraging legislation to reduce, phase out, and even ban the use of plastic packaging and products. The American Plastics Council (APC) came to the rescue with a flashy advertising campaign to inform the public about the substantial efforts the industry was making toward recycling and reuse, and that products and packaging made of plastic actually saved resources compared to other alternatives such as paper or metal. Millions were spent, expectations were high, but success was nowhere to be found. Directly attacking the concerns of the Hate Group didn't convince anyone and ultimately led to the APC being ordered by a dozen or so state attorneys general to desist in their "false" advertising claims about the availability of plastics recycling or else. The APC failed because managers ignored the Love Group in favor of attacking the Hate Group, but they learned their lesson. The next round of ads highlighted the noble qualities of plastics—personal safety and health—that researchers had identified in personal interviews with plastics loyalists. This time the positive results were staggering. Tens of millions of Swing Group households jumped on the plastics bandwagon, positive media coverage outweighed negative media coverage by a two-to-one margin, anti-plastics legislation was pulled, and plastics usage hit all-time highs. Entrepreneurs need to discover what politicians have known for generations, the Love Group holds the keys to victory.

I Don't Have a Love Group, Now What?

Aspiring and established entrepreneurs like the simple Love-Swing-Hate approach to attacking the marketplace, but often point out that their new products, many of which are just in the idea stage, don't have a Love Group. They raise an important point and put themselves on the threshold of discovering what really sets a successful entrepreneur apart from a frustrated would-be entrepreneur. Successful entrepreneurs don't expect their Love Group to find them: they aggressively seek out their Love Group. "Build it and they will come" rarely works in today's world of information overload and product proliferation. Realizing we don't have a Love Group is the first step in beginning to prospect to find a Love Group.

There are many ways to prospect for a Love Group, but we suggest bringing eight to 12 people together that should benefit from the new product, feeding them pizza, and soliciting their impressions. After explaining the product concept, ask questions like, "Who would love this product? What would they love about it? Where and how would they use it?" Or if a little more adventuresome, you might hand out some paper and crayons and ask everyone to draw a picture of someone really loving the product. Then as people show off their artwork, ask questions like, "Who are they; what are they doing; why are they so happy?" Listen and note the responses, but more importantly, observe the participants and look for those few who are completely engaged and articulate. Ask them back to find out more, because they are your Love Group. One prospecting session will not be enough to establish a detailed profile for the Love Group. In our experience, about three to five prospecting sessions are needed, and they should be spread across a variety of geographic regions.

Sometimes prospecting doesn't yield much gold. If that happens, then it is time for some careful reflection and deep thinking. Do I need to change my message? Do I need to change my market? Do I need to set this product aside for a time and pursue another opportunity? There is no reason to give up. The ability to keep on going is what sets entrepreneurs apart from mere mortals!

You're My Love Group, Because I Say You Are!

Sometimes prospecting turns to thoughts of exerting personal pressure, manipulation, and coercion. Levi Strauss provides our favorite corporate example of prospector turned tyrant. In the 1980s, Levi Strauss decided they should manufacture and market a line of three-piece suits called Levi Tailored Classics. At the time, executives wanted to branch out into new areas of clothing over concerns that too high a percentage of their sales came from jeans. They wanted to grow by penetrating new markets.

Levi Strauss did their homework. They examined suit-buying preferences, shopping practices, lifestyles, and demographics for 2,000 men. They uncovered five distinct segments in the market: the traditionalist, the classic independent, the utilitarian, the trendy casual, and the price shopper. The marketing quickly focused in on the "classic independent" as the target, i.e., Love Group. The segment accounted for 21% of male shoppers. They purchased about one-half of men's natural-fiber clothing products, were not price-sensitive, generally shopped for clothes in specialty stores, and strongly preferred tailored clothing rather than buying it off the rack. The Levi Tailored Classics marketing team put together focus groups of the classic independents to prove the new product concept.

The focus group testing went well until it was suggested that (1) the suits would be sold off the rack, and (2) the suits would be manufactured by Levi Strauss. At that point objections flew hot and heavy. Behind the mirror in the focus group facility, the marketing team had answers for every objection. The marketing team pushed forward, even though the product was completely inconsistent with everyone's existing belief about the brand and trounced every physical and emotional benefit these customers wanted because of it. The marketing team picked their Love Group and were determined that their love offerings would be eagerly accepted and appreciated. But predictably, their love was unrequited and the product launch went down in flames.

One would think that entrepreneurs would have more sense than the Levi Strauss marketing team. But again and again we see the same behavior from entrepreneurs dead set on selling to a particular type of customer. They settle for fool's gold rather than prospecting for real gold. To make the point, consider the case of an entrepreneur who had invented a device to measure the curvature and other features of human spinal columns. His technology could give doctors the lowdown on our backbones. Medical doctors, however, are a difficult group. They are highly educated, opinionated, and slow to revise best practices. This didn't stop our entrepreneur. MDs would love his invention, he just knew it. He aggressively pursued them. He pushed hard. They pushed back. They preferred X-rays.

> ## BOOM
> ──THOUGHT 3.9──
>
> *Don't spurn a Love Group, because you may never find another. Once you find customers that love your product, go out and sell to more people just like them.*

In the meantime, chiropractors discovered the new back-measuring device and loved it. It was just what they needed to get a quick read on a new patient's spinal column and to provide feedback on the progress being made by returning patients. The entrepreneur, however, didn't want to sell to chiropractors. He felt they weren't professionals and that their involvement would diminish the seriousness and significance of his invention. He ignored the Love Group, unsuccessfully tried over and over again to sell his invention to the Hate Group, and ultimately squandered hundreds of thousands of investment dollars. The venture went bankrupt. Life is funny. We don't choose love, love chooses us. Entrepreneurs need to be careful not to force love on anyone, but if they do, to be ready to pay the price.

Don't Fight, Don't Appease, Just Bounce

Once we watched a colleague conduct a prospecting session for a product idea he was promoting. He had all of the proper training.

He had completed many successful prospecting sessions in the past. But this time it was different. It was his product idea that people were chewing up and spitting out. He couldn't stay detached. He took every comment personally. He started to argue with session participants who couldn't see the merit of his obviously great idea.

As one might imagine, the spectacle of watching a session moderator arguing with the session participants is not a pretty sight. Any possibility of identifying something helpful and positive was sidetracked. Any hope of finding one or two members of the Love Group was gone. Amid all the fighting, most of the session participants just looked on quietly, wondering when they'd be able to go home and whether they dared eat one or two more cookies while they were waiting to find out. Entrepreneurs want to protect their baby. For them, taking on the Hate Group is a special challenge and personal calling. Unfortunately, it is a waste of time that raises questions among the Love Group, alienates the Swing Group, and empowers the Hate Group.

When confronted with disagreements over the merits of their "baby," entrepreneurs have three courses of action from which to choose. They can appease, fight, or bounce. Said another way, they can grovel and simply say, "You are right," to the criticism and move on to another topic; they can be defensive and lash out at the criticism; or they can use the criticism as a springboard for bouncing their product idea to new heights. We suggest the bounce. Next time someone takes a shot at your "baby," stay in control and improve your chances for success by doing something a little unexpected. Why not smile, play along with the critics, have some fun, and keep probing for million-dollar solutions with flash and panache?

Best Practice: Build Positive Mojo

Sooner or later, we need to consider our employees. Startups can't succeed, regardless of the quality of their horses, without the right team of employees. Seek out people with limitless energy and passion for making things happen. Young businesses need more doers than dreamers, more overachievers than industry stars, more positive mojo than negative stinko.

Every two years, two 12-man teams that represent the best golfers in the US and Europe face off in the Ryder Cup. Every two years, sports analysts say the US has the stronger players. Every two years, the Europeans usually find a way to win and win convincingly. Former US Open Champion and US Ryder Cup player Johnny Miller says we suffer these embarrassing losses because compared to the European team, the US team doesn't have much positive mojo. We agree.

Having stronger players does not guarantee victory in the Ryder Cup or in startup companies. On the other hand, having lots of positive mojo usually does. Positive mojo is the special magical quality that means no doubt, no negativity, no personal power plays, and only positive forward momentum.

Author Jim Collins says great companies get the right people on the bus and get them in the right seats. No argument there, but just what constitutes a *right* person and how such a person can be identified are up for debate. In many startups we've observed, entrepreneurs are happy to just find people willing to get on the bus!

> # BOOM
> THOUGHT 3.10
>
> *Like other employers, entrepreneurs would like to get the right people into the right seats, but often have a hard time just getting people on the "bus" and must make the very most of every employee they have.*

The Art of Resume Reading

Where does positive mojo show up on a resume or in a job interview? We take a very practical approach. We look for "have done" rather than "can do" on a candidate's resume. Often we see resumes listing all sorts of impressive skills and abilities—lots of "can do." However, we don't pay much attention to all the "can do" unless it is accompanied by lots of "have done." We want to see cold, hard evidence that the job candidate has the energy and passion to get things done. The "have done" list may not even have a lot to do with the current job opening. That's fine! Perhaps even better! We want a doer who has the knack for generating success wherever they go. Of course, we also look for someone with at least a touch of personal charm and charisma. We want a positive mojo generator that has a positive click with the team. Startup companies need someone who creates energy rather than someone who just consumes energy.

HR recruiters at Fortune 500 companies rarely, if ever, look for positive mojo. They want world-class pedigree. They want relevant job experience. They want up-to-date skills and top-of-class ranking. They want someone they feel comfortable with, but who may be least likely to have anything positive going on with the business team looking for the new hire. We feel "hiring the best athlete" is an expensive and risky way to hire, particularly for startups, and are not surprised by studies showing that within five years, two-thirds of MBAs leave their first job, with an astounding one out of five switching employers twice. Startups cannot weather all the drama of *getting the wrong people off the bus.* Hire positive mojo—that is, hire people who bring positive energy to the group and have some magic for getting things done.

Definitely Not "All in the Family"

One would think that going into business with family and friends creates a lot of positive mojo. After all, family members and friends enjoy close ties and share years of happy memories. Surprisingly, we haven't seen much in the way of positive mojo from such situations. Quite the contrary: going into business with family and friends often proves to be a never ending wellspring of negative no-go mojo. Consider one example of many we could share.

Once we were invited to consult with a small family-owned company that manufactures kit sports cars. They had some questions about their product development and pricing policies. To put the company in perspective, we'd describe the five partners as a passionate engineer, a charismatic visionary and salesman, a bright but sulky grump going along for the ride, a well-intentioned but dish-it-out dad wanting to help his sons build a successful business, and a loving mom trying to hold all the pieces together. Once we arrived at their business, it was painfully evident that we were invited to help fight the battles for one brother versus the other two brothers with the mom acting as referee. Needless to say, our time with the startup wasn't very productive. We knew that no matter what advice we offered, the salesman brother would have his way, the engineer brother would be satisfied that "experts"

> **BOOM**
> ──THOUGHT 3.11──
>
> *Hiring family and friends is a great idea, right? Wrong! Building a company around family and friends usually destroys mojo. Take their investment money, but not their job applications.*

supported his point of view, and the grumpy brother would still be grumpy.

Thinking about it, it must be the rare pair of siblings who enjoy working together for long hours, in tense conditions, and with personal futures and a lot of money on the line. Often it takes a considerable amount of time for a startup to be successful, and when several months pass without the business progressing as hoped, family and friends can start to bicker about the *right* direction for the company, who isn't making a *fair* contribution, or who isn't getting *fair* compensation. Relationships with family members and friends are too valuable to sacrifice to the gods of entrepreneurship. Don't make your startup company a fractured Family Affair.

Team Mojo

Every entrepreneur wants to put together a dream team. They want to cherry-pick industry stars to join the team and drive their startup company to victory. Bad idea! Dream teams rarely deliver. Often they don't have mojo. More winning dynasties are forged out of working-class overachievers than overhyped dream-teamers with set ideas on what customers want and how businesses should deliver it.

Entrepreneurs really need a do-team rather than a dream team. Do-teams are much more challenging to assemble than dream-teams. Like the dream team, do-teams have gifted and talented people. Yet, their modest egos allow them to work together without each striving for the limelight or an extraordinary personal bonanza. When building with mojo, put together a team that naturally strives for what economists call Nash Equilibrium. That is, a mindset in which each team member works together to go for something good rather than having each team member put themselves first and fight for the single best personal payoff. Based on our experience, teams with a cooperative, everyone-wins mindset usually succeed. On the other hand, uncooperative, self-seeking teams ultimately turn everyone away empty-handed.

Do-teams find a way to put aside competing agendas. As an example, consider a group of entrepreneurs building a tennis club out in Idaho. Frustrated with poor results at their tennis club, the entrepreneurs invited a local tennis star to give them some advice. The tennis star didn't know much about entrepreneurial startups, but as a stand-out athlete, he knew a lot about positive mojo. Consequently, before giving out any answers he first asked a question, "What kind of a club do you want—that is, what kind of a club would you be excited to be part of?"

The entrepreneurs spent the next half-hour discussing whether they wanted an exclusive club, a family-oriented club, or a club for students and other local-area singles. In another half-hour, with the positive mojo building, they concluded that they all would be excited to be part of an exclusive tennis club. Now with some excitement and a clear vision behind their efforts, they easily answered the remaining questions about appropriate pricing, promotional tools, people to target, and club improvements to make. Team Mojo saved the day and the club went on to success.

Don't Just Sell . . . Evangelize Team Mojo

Successful startups are built with a team of believers! Do-teams approach a business venture like it is a single-minded mission from on high. They don't just build and sell, they evangelize! When you have a do-team of five believers, you get the momentum and productivity mojo of 10 employees. Unfortunately, the opposite is also true. When you have four believers and one nonbeliever, you lose momentum and only get the equivalent productivity of one employee.

Successful entrepreneurs have the knack of quickly weeding out nonbelievers to keep the mojo high. "Slow to hire and quick to fire" is their motto for protecting team mojo.

We believe that startups have their best chance for success when management gives credit to their employees instead of taking all the credit for themselves. There are two types of cultures we find in most new ventures: me-oriented and we-oriented. In the first culture, the CEO or top VPs take credit for every award and accolade that comes their way. Basically they say, "Look at me—ain't I great?" People in me-oriented cultures focus on "What's in it for me?" and everyone looks to maximize their own wealth and their own star status at the expense of the overall good of the company. Me-oriented cultures tear down Team Mojo and in the long term, may even completely destroy it.

In contrast, we-oriented cultures make it a habit to generously recognize and credit the teams that successfully do the day-to-day work inside the company. In these cultures, the CEO consistently recognizes the employees who make the venture possible. When the focus moves from "CEO takes all credit" to "Give credit where credit is due," magically employee attitudes change from "What's in it for me?" to "How can we work together for success?" When employees are looking for ways to work together to succeed rather than looking for ways to maximize their own personal returns while minimizing their personal efforts, it is much easier to tackle the tough problems facing new ventures. Team Mojo helps start-ups accelerate their growth exponentially. The culture of your new venture is clearly a choice. Please make the choice for we-oriented culture.

Review Questions

Define with Five

Define the following vocabulary words using five words or less.

1. Horses

   _____

2. Benefactor

   _____

3. Anchor Customer

   _____

4. Reference Price

   _____

5. We-Oriented Culture

   _____

Question the Answer

Answer each phrase below in the form of a question.

1. Learning to leverage the efforts of others.

   _____

2. The answer to this question is the key to finding initial investors, partners, and anchor customers.

   _____

3. The type of customers that help startups get past the difficult first steps of doing business.

_____

4. The three "lowest common denominators" of entrepreneurship.

_____

5. The question all aspiring entrepreneurs must be able to answer about their customers.

_____

Smarter than an Entrepreneur

Name the product or venture that reinforces or violates a Boom Start best practice.

1. Beat the commodity carpet pricing game by finding benefactors down the value chain.

_____

2. Proved that even innovative, time-saving designs can be commercial failures when they don't fit with our current way of doing things.

_____

3. Flunked the usability test by forcing customers to type with a tiny "Chiclet" keyboard.

_____

4. Went from rabbits to riches by putting good-sized stores in one-horse towns that other retailers ignored.

_____

5. Found smooth sailing once they pulled two anchors, Microsoft and eBay, on board.

_____

SuperLaws in Action

Identifying Benefactors for your startup is a key to finding initial investors, partners, and anchor customers. Benefactors win when you win!

Activity: Describe a startup business and its business model. Next, identify three potential Benefactors and explain how they win when the startup business wins.

Describe the business:

Describe the business model:

Benefactor	How they win when startup wins

chapter 4 Play Big

Surround yourself with reputable people, ideas, and companies.
Find ways to look big and play big, even if you're not big.

The puffer fish is a fascinating creature. It has the ability to look big, even when it's not. In a relaxed state, the puffer fish seems relatively normal. When threatened, however, the puffer fish undergoes a remarkable transformation. The puffer fish actually pumps water into its stomach, which expands to nearly a hundred times its original volume. This is made possible by the unique pleats in the stomach. The body then swells to approximately three times its usual size, thanks to the skin's elasticity. As you might imagine, this transformation has a powerful effect on potential predators.

The puffer fish's amazing transformation has important implications for entrepreneurs. Think about your situation. Although you have created uniquely differentiated products for carefully selected customers, you are competing against bigger companies—big in terms of money, resources, personnel, and image. And customers associate big with safe. "It's safe to do business with this company because it is *big*." "Big Blue," aka IBM, made a living on the image of "big" for years. But you are a small startup company. How do you compete with the "big boys?" How do customers and investors perceive your new business?

1. Customers want to see a stable company, but you are not established.
2. Advisors want to work with a viable company, but you are not proven.

3. Suppliers want to partner with the industry standard, but you are a niche player.
4. Partners want to team up with a reputation builder, but you don't have a "blue chip" track record.

Do you want to look like the uninflated puffer fish, scrawny and weak, or do you want to look like the plus-sized puffer fish, sturdy and strong? Find ways to play big, even if you're not. Look for ways to level the playing field. You do this with people, ideas, relationships, and technology.

People

To play big, surround yourself with reputable people. Get "the right people on the bus and then figure out where to drive it," says Jim Collins, author of *Good to Great*.[1] Who, you might ask, are the right people? For entrepreneurs, the answer is people who can help you grow your business. Because that answer is a bit vague, we'll turn to Malcolm Gladwell, author of *The Tipping Point*, for clarity. Gladwell asserts that the best way to understand how populations adopt and use new products and services is to think of products as epidemics. "Ideas and products and messages and behaviors spread just like viruses do."[2] And, according to Gladwell, there are three types of people who can facilitate, even accelerate, the spread of your product/service among customers—connectors, mavens, and salespeople.

Connectors are people specialists. They have an extraordinary ability to make friends and new acquaintances across a variety of business, social, and cultural worlds. Further, they have the capacity—mental, social, and physical—to maintain a myriad of casual acquaintances. Because of their intrinsic sociability traits, such as personality, self-confidence, and curiosity, connectors know a lot of people and they know a variety of people. "We rely on them to give us access to opportunities and worlds to which we don't belong."[3] A connector's Rolodex means potentially big opportunities for entrepreneurs. So, think of the

[1] *Good to Great*, by Jim Collins (New York: Harper Business, 2001)
[2] *The Tipping Point*, by Malcolm Gladwell (New York: Back Bay Books/Little, Brown and Company, 2002)
[3] Ibid.

connectors you know. They have lots of friends and acquaintances. They work, play, and socialize in many different worlds. Because of this, they can play a significant role in "connecting" you to the right people: customers, suppliers, distributors, investors, etc.

Mavens are information specialists. Just as connectors connect people to people, mavens connect people to the marketplace with information. Mavens have high interest in collecting information about products, prices, and places. But this is not all. More importantly, they want to share this information with others. We all have our own sets of market mavens. For example, think of a time when you wanted to purchase a new consumer electronics product. Whom did you turn to for information? We look to our colleague and friend Craig, who voraciously reads anything written about cameras, phones, music systems, GPS, etc. In our minds, if Craig does not know, nobody knows. For us, he is the expert, the person we turn to for information and advice. According to Gladwell, and we agree, "mavens have the knowledge and the social skills to start word-of-mouth epidemics."[4] With that power of influence, entrepreneurs should seek out these market mavens and provide them with information. Think of the potential impact this could have on your business—a word-of-mouth epidemic about your product.

Salespeople are the persuaders! So, connectors link people to people, mavens connect people to information, and salespeople persuade people to do something. Without salespeople, some potential customers may never act; they may never purchase. They have to be persuaded. Indeed, a Harvard Business School study identified face-to-face selling as an important determinant of success for new ventures.[5] Learn to sell. If you can't, find someone who can.

So, if you want to be the plus-sized puffer fish, surround yourself with the right people: connectors, mavens, and salespeople.

Ideas

To play big, surround yourself with great ideas. Nolan Bushnell, considered by many to be the father of the video game industry,

[4] Ibid.
[5] *The Road Well Traveled*, by Amar Bhide (Harvard Business School Press, June 12, 1998)

founder of Atari and the Chuck E. Cheese's Pizza-Time Theaters chain, notes that having a new idea isn't necessarily new: "Everyone who's ever taken a shower has an idea. It's the person who gets out of the shower, dries off and does something about it who makes a difference."

So, make a difference. Do something about your great ideas. Find ways to communicate them to potential customers. In the early days of Covey Leadership, Steven Covey and a small group of consultants began teaching the principles they had collected and developed over the previous 20 years. It was a small organization with seminars and consulting projects in approximately five major cities. They muddled along for a few years until they found a big way to communicate their great ideas. The best thing this group did, according to Covey, was write *Seven Habits of Highly Effective People,* which became a national bestseller. They communicated their big ideas to potential customers. "The book became a real 'Trojan Horse,'" said Covey. "It opened up doors in unbelievable ways. It had legs of its own." The success of the book created buzz disproportionate to the size of the company and generated significant publicity for the consulting business.

Now, you don't have to write a book, but you do need to find ways to communicate your big ideas to the market. One way to do this is to write articles or press releases for trade publications, magazines, and newspapers. Simon Jacomet, founder of Zai, a Swiss ski manufacturer, discovered the benefits of publicity early on. "Zai," a Romansh word meaning tough or resistant, fits well the Swiss ski company that produces extraordinary handmade skis at a price tag of SFr3,300 ($2,700) a pair. Founded in 2003, Jacomet and his team started with little marketing budget, but had an interesting story to tell. The story was about a group of craftsmen in the tiny town of Disentis, Switzerland, who used state-of-the-art high-tech materials to construct skis by hand. And tell the story they did. They told the story to ski and sport magazines: *Drive, Fit for Fun, Outside Magazine, Skipresse, Skitime.* But this was not all. They focused on publications that would reach their target market: skiers with money and people with money. They told their story in such publications as *Architectural Digest, Amica, Bella, Best Fashion, Elle Decoration, Europa, Finest Clubs, Finest Finance, Four Seasons, GQ, Ideat, Maison Française, Newsweek, Optimum, Panorama, Paris Match, Quote, Robb Report, Stocks, Style Journal, Styletto, Swiss Universe,* and *Ticino Management,* to name a few. These efforts resulted in significant interest among customers in this high-end market. In fact one customer, a non-skier, purchased a pair of skis as a showpiece, just to carry around in his Rolls-Royce.

Similarly, in the early days of Dentrix, Andy Jensen, director of marketing, spent a good portion of his time writing articles for dental publications and for professional dental associations. He found many editors starving for interesting articles. This relatively free advertising was like gold for Dentrix in the early days of the company.

The great ideas of Covey Leadership, Zai, and Dentrix, combined with targeted publicity, helped these new ventures make a splash in the marketplace. Because their ideas looked big, they played big, like the puffer fish, like viable players.

Companies

To play big, surround yourself with great companies. Whom you associate with says a lot to potential customers. You've heard of guilt by association. This is respect by association. You bring respect or credibility to your company by whom you associate with. But don't get a big head by working with big companies. This sort of credibility is only temporary. A big company is like your fairy godmother that can grant you greatness long enough for you to go to the big dance and meet Prince Charming. But after you meet the prince, you are on your own. To keep and build credibility, you have to earn it on your own. And to earn credibility, you have to deliver results to your customers. "Customers, like banks, will take a first chance on you if you come backed by the best. But they will not do so a second time, *no matter how glowing your references,* unless you prove your own personal reliability with results."[6]

Strut Your Stuff, Look Your Best, Play to Your Strengths

Now, playing big is important, but you have to do more than look big. You have to look your best. Consider the male sage grouse, for example. He fans his tail feathers, inflates his gular air sac, and

---

[6] *The New Conceptual Selling,* by Stephen E. Heiman, Diane Sanchez, and Tad Tueja (New York: Warner Books, 1999)

makes popping sounds, all to compete for the attention of females during the spring courtship ritual. This turns into a spectacular show for the ladies as the males try to stand out and look their best. You can imagine that the male who shows up with a deflated breast, no tail feathers, and no popping sound walks away with no companion. And so it is with new ventures. If you want to attract the attention of potential customers, strut your stuff. Show off what you do well. We call this "playing to your strength." But playing to your strength in front of the wrong group of potential customers, or worse, no audience at all, is useless. The male sage grouse struts his stuff in a display area called a lek. This is where the females gather to watch. Strutting in other places yields no results. So, play to your strength in the right place—in front of the right customers.

Technology—Just Google Me

A new wave of technology is leveling the playing field, enabling entrepreneurs to play big. Just look around. With today's technology, and who knows what's in store for tomorrow, a startup company can have a website presence on the Internet, make itself accessible, analyze and optimize information, manage e-commerce with fully integrated store and back-office functions, monitor vendors halfway around the world, and deploy world-class logistics services. It was just a few years ago that only the big companies could access and afford these tools. Today, technology has become the great leveler, giving entrepreneurs and new ventures the ability to compete with big business. "It's never been easier to play big."[7]

Danger Ahead

Inappropriately "playing big" can lead to danger or even business decline and failure! "Playing big" is not about fooling, tricking, or deceiving the market. It is not about lying, telling half-truths, bending agreements, or manipulating financials. It is simply about looking big, in a reputable way. Honesty is always the best policy, but when doing business, honesty is an absolute necessity! Once

---

[7]"Small Companies That Play Big," by Julie Sloane, Justin Martin, and Alessandra Bianchi, in *Fortune Small Business*, Vol. 16, No. 9 (November 1, 2006)

trust is lost among business partners and customers, it is very difficult to regain.

Remember the old adage, "Fool me once, shame on you; fool me twice, shame on me." This isn't about fooling the marketplace. For as soon as the firm loses its reputation, it loses business. And where there is no business, there is no company. So, be careful. Surround yourself with reputable people, ideas, and companies. Play to your strengths. Capitalize on technology. Learn to play big, even if you are not.

BOOM
-----THOUGHT 4.1-----

Watch out or you may go from puffer fish to fish bait. Playing big is not about fooling or tricking. It is about finding ways to act big in meaningful, legitimate ways.

Best Practice: Feed a Frenzy

A fear of being at a competitive disadvantage or a lost business opportunity provide a strong incentive for people to get involved. If you want to get distributors, partners, investors, and key customers to sell, champion, invest in, or buy your angle, create a feeding frenzy by following the Rule of Three.

Sharks have the same senses people have, including taste, touch, eyesight, hearing, and smell. However, a shark's primary sense is smell. It can detect one drop of blood in a million drops of water and can smell blood a quarter of a mile away. When sharks smell blood in the water and see others circling their food, they go crazy biting anything around them. In short, seeing the opportunity to feed and watching other sharks circle the food gets them excited about the feeding opportunity and creates an insatiable appetite. When sharks get into a feeding frenzy, they close their eyes and go for it!

You don't have to scuba dive to experience a feeding frenzy. People exhibit the same pattern as sharks. Each year, especially around Thanksgiving and Christmas, shoppers become very excited when presented with the opportunity for a bargain. When the loudspeakers in a store trumpet, "Bargain in aisle five," watch shoppers run to the location, snapping up products they hadn't planned on with an insatiable appetite. When Christmas sales are advertised in the newspaper, watch people line up the night before just to be first in line to run through the store like crazy sharks, circling every bargain and attacking everything and anything around them.

One of the best descriptions of a human feeding frenzy is contained in a report written in *The Tech Online Edition* on May 9th, 2000 about MIT students during a freshman orientation:

I started contemplating this after attending the recent Class of 2002 Ring Delivery. Following a reception (with food) at Killian Court, sophomores were bused to the harbor. Immediately after boarding the cruise ship, students found themselves in a huge crowd vaguely resembling a line. Apparently more free food lay ahead. There, all hell broke loose. Picture 800 students forming a mob in order to get to two tables of various desserts. The scene resembled a mosh pit. Any sense of order which might have been present initially was soon lost as everyone swarmed around the tables. Pushing and shoving ensued in a battle to reach the food faster. Some people walked off with plates loaded with goodies, as others received none. Those in the back of the crowd couldn't reach the tables; those who had taken their share of food couldn't find room to leave the area amidst the mob scene. People began passing trays of food from the tables to the back of the crowd in order to satisfy them, but this soon ceased as the trays broke with so many grabbing for them. It was one of the most greedy, primitive displays I've ever seen.

While we know what drives a feeding frenzy in sharks, why do people exhibit the same primitive pattern? Answer: because of the FUG factor.

F: Fear of losing out on an opportunity; don't like others getting the deal on the "Wow Angle" before them.

U: Uncertainty if the opportunity will come their way again; don't want to miss out on the opportunity of a "Wow Angle."

G: Greed; people want an opportunity to hit the jackpot with a "Wow Angle."

Thus, instead of blood in the water, it is fear, uncertainty, and greed that spark the feeding frenzy in distributors, retailers, partners, and customers. Don't just allow one shark to circle your angle. With one shark in the water, the only thing that will get bitten is your company.

Never, never, never allow one key stakeholder to hold your company hostage. Great angles will attract the attention of many other sharks. Allow others to see, smell, or even taste your angle. With startup companies, we find it is human nature for people to take action only when they are motivated to do so by the FUG factor. As entrepreneurs, we don't have the time to wait for distributors, partners, and investors to eventually wake up and then make up their minds. Time is money and startup companies have a limited amount of time to survive. Don't just allow the "special few" to view your angle. Go ahead and show as many people as possible your angle. You will be glad you did. To get results, encourage the feeding frenzy when the opportunity comes your way.

The Rule of Three: Three Reasons to Take Action

The ABCs of a feeding frenzy follow the Rule of Three. The Rule of Three is based on the idea that it takes a minimum of three people swimming around your angle to get someone to take immediate action. Many entrepreneurs are so excited about finally finding a willing partner, investor, or distributor that they usually "give in" to unreasonable demands or "give up" future opportunities to make money in order to seal a deal. You don't have to do that. If you are going to survive and thrive as a company, you must allow a minimum of three people to swim around your angle. To do otherwise is *success-a-cide*. Unfortunately, it is all too common for us to hear the following statements by entrepreneurs:

> *To start our company, we want to work closely with just your group.*
>
> *We are not talking with anyone else except you because we value your relationship.*
>
> *We want to give you exclusive rights so that you will have a competitive position in the marketplace.*

How noble yet naïve these entrepreneurs are. The above statements reflect common tactics tried by inexperienced startups. Unfortunately, such tactics are doomed to fail and kill any feeding frenzy to propel your new company to success. When you don't allow others to view and compete for your product, you do not motivate partners or buyers to take action. Hence, no FUG factor, no

The Rule of Three

Have at least three sharks biting on your business opportunity in order to increase your chances for success!

© 2009, JupiterImages

contracts, and limited sales. Such mindsets of fledgling entrepreneurs give key customers no reason to take action. We have seen time and time again that when there is no feeding frenzy, there is little need to take action and contracts stall, inventory sits, and sales falter.

We want key customers, like sharks, to get excited about the opportunities in front of them. We have seen deals that go on for years change in a minute when other distributors, partners, and investors are brought into the picture. Like sharks, people get more excited about opportunities when they see others swimming around.

The level of excitement and appetite for a deal increases as others look at, sample, and negotiate for your angle. Feeding frenzies begin with at least three interested parties. With a minimum of three circling your angle, watch how distributors, investors, and partners begin snapping up your terms and quickly move toward the close. When this happens, congratulations: you just witnessed FUG in action—a true feeding frenzy.

Stopping the Frenzy Is Futile: Let Them Bite or Get Bitten

In 2007, no product received more press than the launch of the Apple iPhone. Unlike other Apple products, the iPhone was the result of an exclusive partnership between Apple and AT&T. In order to purchase an Apple iPhone, consumers must commit to being an AT&T customer for two years. Many analysts wonder why Apple made exclusive arrangements with AT&T and limited their opportunity to sell the phone on all wireless platforms. Clearly this violates the Rule of Three. It is very frustrating to consumers when they can see, hear, and touch an iPhone but not buy it because they already carry a two-year contract with T-Mobile or Sprint. Perhaps it is unwise to restrict a feeding frenzy. All that snapping energy has to go somewhere.

Within a year of the product launch, a class-action lawsuit was filed in federal court targeting Apple and AT&T. The lawsuit accuses the companies of illegally conspiring to tie iPhone customers to the telecommunications company's wireless network. The suit seeks around $2 billion in damages.

According to lawyers for Paul A. Holman in Washington State, Apple and AT&T conspired to block all modifications of Apple's iPhone to stymie any attempt by users or competitors to diminish or tap into the Apple-AT&T revenue stream. When a great angle attracts national attention, it is probably unwise to stop a feeding frenzy. When people circle an angle they like and want, but can't get, someone is going to get bitten. In this case, it may be the hand that feeds.

The power of a great angle is its ability to create excitement with distributors, partners, investors, and key customers. If we follow the experience of successful entrepreneurs, using the Rule of Three will vastly multiply our opportunities to grow. Allowing only one shark to swim around your angle probably means that your company is the only one that gets hurt.

Best Practice: Be an Underdog

Number two may be big, but they still try harder! Inject energy into your startup by tapping into the power of the underdog and

BOOM
─THOUGHT 4.2─

Tap into the power of the underdog. America loves the underdog because they know that #2 really does work harder!

start enjoying the brash "in your face" freedom that being the underdog affords.

"Hello there. My name is Fred Bartles and this is Ed Jaymes. You know, it occurred to Ed the other day that between his fruit orchard and my premium-grade wine vineyard, we could make a truly superior premium-grade wine cooler. It sounded good to me. So Ed took out a second on his house, and wrote to Harvard for an MBA, and now we're preparing to enter the wine cooler business. We will try to keep you posted on how it's going. And thank you for your business."

If you were in the market for a wine cooler in the 1980s, you definitely wanted to check out Bartles & Jaymes. It had to be good. It was made by two old farmers doing their very best to make their customers happy. They didn't know anything about big business or all the other fancy stuff that Harvard MBAs can do. They just knew how to work hard and put out a good product. They had a lot at stake. Poor Ed had to find a way to please customers. He had put a second mortgage on his house to start his business.

However, there never were a real Bartles and a real Jaymes. The two old farmers were just two old actors. Bartles & Jaymes wine coolers were manufactured and marketed by Ernest & Julio Gallo, the largest wine producer in the world.

Bartles and Jaymes were so successful at selling wine coolers back in the 80s that Gallo is thinking of bringing them back now, more than 20 years later, to sell a new line of products. The Bartles & Jaymes concept succeeds in America because we love the underdog and believe the underdog deserves a chance, but also because we know from experience that the underdog does indeed work extra hard.

Underdog Power

In a commencement address, former Vice President Dick Cheney observed, "One of the things I love most about our country is that we have such opportunities. America is still the country of a second chance. Most of us end up needing one." He then went on to share experiences from his life that showed he had several second chances in his career and how his success came from opportunities he least expected. The speech returned rousing applause and a standing ovation. America loves giving second chances as much as it loves the underdog.

If you can't be #1, then embrace #2. Most everyone is familiar with Avis Car Rental. Avis is #2 and proud of it. Their advertising copy says, "We try harder." Now, that is a brash statement, but nobody minds, because #2 is the underdog and consumers feel good about doing business with a group of people that "try harder."

As an entrepreneur, leverage your smallness! You want to be an underdog that does business with other underdogs. We've observed that new businesses often want the reassurance of doing business with #1. However, the reassurance and prestige of working with the market leader can be costly. Outside the world of entrepreneurs, customers buy from IBM because "no one ever got fired for buying from IBM," buy DuPont's "red oval," buy Dow Chemical's "red diamond," buy Xerox's "customer support," and so forth. Each of these companies charges a premium, but do they deliver greater value than lesser companies? While entrepreneurs should work with one or two credibility-building large companies, they should also remember to buy performance rather than bling: hard work and commitment rather than size and comfort.

"In Your Face" Underdogs

Allegiance is an underdog and proud of it. Providing software and questionnaires for analyzing employee and customer engagement with a company, the business was put together by an unlikely alliance between a 50-something business school professor and a 20-something accounting grad.

Underdogs can be aggressive and we love them for it. Allegiance hired a hungry sales team, relentlessly makes cold calls, and attends all the key tradeshows. Even their software is aggressive. Focusing on retail banking and telecommunications, Allegiance stresses real-time analysis and feedback, while pointing out that most of their competitors take months to provide their analysis and feedback. By then, so the co-founders say, "the freight train has already run over the business."

According to Gartner Group analysts, Allegiance products are superior to their much bigger and much pricier competitors. Underdog startups can turn heads and generate buzz by doing things that would go unnoticed or even raise eyebrows if coming from bigger, more established businesses.

Best Practice: Hatch a Catchphrase

Don't underestimate the power of a jingle or a few carefully selected and memorable words when playing big. A great catchphrase keeps your product strategy focused and focuses buyers on key product benefits. Catchphrases sell products.

Let's play a game. When we mention a catchphrase, we want you to think of the first product that comes top-of-mind. Here we go—the catchphrases are: "Reach out and touch someone," "It's everywhere you want to be," "The ultimate driving machine," "When you care enough to send the very best," and "M'm! M'm! Good!" Did you first think of AT&T, Visa, BMW, Hallmark Cards, and Campbell's Soup? If so, then you are thinking along the same lines as the majority of Americans. Each of these Hall of Fame catchphrases brings to mind a focused, well-defined image, which in turn brings to mind a focused, well-defined brand. When we consider buying one of these brands, the catchphrase helps us remember exactly what we will be getting and exactly why we want it!

What's in a Word—Part One

BOOM
THOUGHT 4.3

Minds can't shake loose a great catchphrase. Catchphrases focus customers on product benefits and focus employees on delivering customer value.

Crafting a memorable catchphrase is becoming a lost art. It has been a long time since catchphrase blockbusters like "Where's the beef," "The real thing," and "You deserve a break today" came down the pike for Wendy's, Coca-Cola, and McDonald's. Can you remember what slogans these brands use today? Most people can't. A recent research study conducted by Emergence, a brand-strategy firm based in Atlanta, found that fewer than half of today's top catchphrases were known by more than 5% of their national sample of consumers. Large companies and advertising agencies apparently have lost sight of the catchphrase's power. They seem to adopt a new phrase each year to match the direction of the ad campaign rather than matching each new ad campaign to their tried-and-true slogan.

Startups that want to *play big* just don't have the financial resources to take a *big business* approach to branding. Entrepreneurs must put their pride aside and focus their business with a catchphrase even if big-time brand managers and advertising creative directors say such things are trite and unsophisticated. Sticking with a great catchphrase gives a startup direction, focus, and market presence. Sticking with a great catchphrase grabs mind share, and growing mind share is a must for startups because more mind share equals more market share.

The High Cost of Not Being Highly Focused

Now let's play another game. Take two or three minutes and list all the consumer electronics brands that you can think of. In a recent survey, over 17,000 consumers rated 15 leading consumer electronics brands. These brands included Apple, Canon, Casio, Dell, Hitachi, Hewlett-Packard, Microsoft, Nokia, Panasonic, Philips, Pioneer, Sanyo, Sharp, Sony, and Toshiba. Incidentally, among the 15 brands listed, Sony was rated as the best and Sanyo as the worst. In your list of brands, did you recall all 15 of the leading brands? Did you happen to think of LG? In fact, when you think LG, does anything come to mind? How about "Lucky Goldstar" or "Life's Good"—still nothing?

LG has been around for a long time, but owns very little mind share in the brains of American consumers. It was formed in 1947 and started making appliances in 1958. Aside from being a leading chemical manufacturer, LG is among the world's biggest makers of digital displays, CD-ROM drives, DVD-ROM drives, recording media, video phones, cell phones, PC cameras, automatic banking systems, air conditioners, refrigerators, microwave ovens, washing machines, vacuum cleaners, compressors, security systems, optical switching devices, building information systems, satellite handsets, mobile multimedia services—well, by now you may be asking yourself, "What don't they make?" It must be very hard to manage a company with such a diverse set of products. With such a company, it is absolutely difficult to project a clear and focused brand image. Sadly, the cost of being unfocused is alarmingly high!

Several years ago we were studying the relationships between pricing, brand names, and sales in the replacement market for CD-ROM drives. To kick off the research, we went to a local computer store with an LG executive to look at their product facings. We were impressed. LG drives dominated the eye-level shelf space. Everywhere we looked on the aisle, there were LG CD-ROM drives. We introduced ourselves to a salesperson and enthusiastically asked about the unit sales for the LG drives compared to the competitive drives. The salesperson slightly frowned and then said that the Creative Labs Sound Blaster drives outsold all other drives, including the LG drive, by more than a two-to-one margin. The executive was shocked and surprised for a couple of reasons. The LG drive was priced at less than two-thirds the cost of the Sound Blaster, and LG, in point of fact, made the drive being sold by Sound Blaster! The executive was frustrated that the technology company LG made all of the computer hardware, but the marketing company Creative Labs made all the profit.

It Weighs 43 Tons and Fires a 2200-Lb. Shell Over Nine Miles

And the question is: what is the Big Bertha, a mobile howitzer designed by the Germans in 1914? Big Bertha is also the perfect name for a golfer's big stick, the driver. Even one year before its introduction, no one would have thought that golfers all around the world would replace their traditional wooden drivers with metal-headed Big Berthas. Did it show up on a Gallup survey that golfers needed drivers with the head size of a small shoebox? On the other hand, Eli Callaway had the technology to make huge metal driver heads, and the Big Bertha driver was born. Sometimes the right brand name can function just like a great catchphrase.

Eli Callaway's Big Bertha drivers were a runaway success, but only because an entrepreneur was willing to take the risk of breaking with over 100 years of golfing tradition. Using robotic golf machines, large metal heads didn't perform any better than small wooden heads with on-center hits. But golf is played by humans and not robots, and even the highly gifted Dumbo needed a magic feather to fly. The big metal head sure looks easier to hit than the tiny wooden ones, who cares if we can't hit the Big Bertha any farther or straighter than with old wooden clubs. We think we can. It is our magic feather. That's what matters. And who can forget the brand name Big Bertha? The name says hugeness, roundness, and power. It has the sort of stick-to-the-mind quality that makes for a *downright dynamite* catchphrase.

Catchphrase 101

The first lesson in Catchphrase 101 is that effective catchphrases are straightforward. They roll off the tongue with rhyme, alliteration, and the "insider perspective" of unpretentious cowboy poetry. But don't be fooled. Just because great catchphrases are simple does not make them simple-minded. Marketing professional and writer Al Ries is believed to have coined the terms "positioning" and "mind share." His advice on writing a catchphrase is to wrap the benefit with bacon. For example, he points out that BMW automobiles own the benefit "fun driving." With that as the benefit, many of us might write the catchphrase, "BMW: it is fun to drive!" The catchphrase is simple and direct, but it isn't wrapped in bacon—that is, that special something to make the phrase memorable and dig a spot into our overloaded brains. Obviously, the highly acclaimed catchphrase "The Ultimate Driving Machine" wraps the BMW benefit in some pretty thick and juicy bacon.

Don't settle on a catchphrase that highlights something that catches your imagination but doesn't stress something that directly benefits your customer. Those types of slogans fail the *simple* test. They require too much mental processing for the customer to get it. For example, Ford Motor Company's "Quality is job one," McDonald's "We love to see you smile," General Electric's "Imagination at work," and Timex's "Life is ticking" express fine sentiment, we think, but may not make a direct connection with the majority of customers. Contrast these poor examples with the classic "You're in good hands with Allstate," the very memorable "Ace is the place with the helpful hardware man," or the all-world mind grabber "Snap! Crackle! Pop! Rice Krispies."

Startups should invest plenty of time and energy identifying a memorable catchphrase and then stick with it for the long term. There is no sense in changing catchphrases like dirty underwear. Change disrupts business focus, confuses customers, and throws away mind share. This lesson is a problem for Fortune 500 companies because they employ ad agencies and creative directors. The trouble is that agencies always want to reinvent and be creative, as that is what they do best. This lesson can be a problem for startups because they often believe a good product will sell itself and they will not spend adequate time developing an effective, mind-grabbing catchphrase.

The power of a slogan can be enhanced by combining it with a powerful brand name. Duracell's catchphrase, "You can't top the copper top," makes a strong benefit statement, but then so does Duracell as a brand name for everyday-use batteries. Other examples are Bounty, "The quicker picker upper," Meow Mix, "Tastes so good that cats ask for it by name," and Federal Express, "When it absolutely, positively has to be there overnight."

What's in a Word—Part Two

To play big, entrepreneurs must multiply the impact of each marketing touch point. In our experience, a great brand name goes hand in hand with a great catchphrase when launching a successful startup. When we think about brand names, we have developed our own unique way of sorting out winners from losers. Great brand names like Häagen-Dazs are invented, not borrowed, and evoke strong emotions and feelings that tap into our imaginations. Häagen-Dazs is an invented word, yet it has a rich and sophisticated European ring to it. Because it is invented, there are no has-

Go for the Light

When naming a brand, stick to invented-benefits and avoid the borrowed-features. The former can be uniquely yours and have a *stickiness* that the latter have a hard time matching. You invented a product; now invent a name to go along with it!

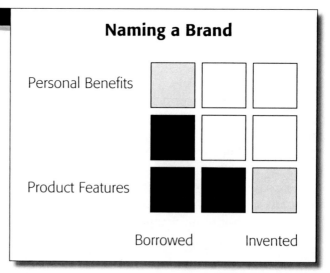

sles with stepping on existing trademarks and brand names. Because it is invented, the brand name only carries the emotional baggage we want. Because it is invented, the brand name can be tuned to evoke the best-for-the-product-category feelings, emotions, moods, and personal evaluations, i.e., differentiating personal benefits.

Brand names like Stainmaster hit in the middle of the grid. Not a name drawn entirely from the imagination, but not your standard dictionary word either. Not a brand that evokes strong emotions and feelings. However, it does give human emotion at least a small tickle, as "mastering stains" is pretty good. The Stainmaster brand name clearly does more than state a product feature using literal, dictionary terms. Great brand names sticking with these ideas are all around us: for example, Pepsi, Charmin, and Google are great. On the other hand, stinko brand names are hard to find but funny when we do: for example, the very literal and product-feature-oriented brand name iSmell, an unsuccessful personal scent synthesizer for Internet odors. As a brand name, iSmell edges out iStink, but only by a nose!

Best Practice: Reach Out with Touch Points

Woo and court customers and investors by identifying and creating touch points. Every interaction, transaction, and engagement is an opportunity to build relationships and strong commitment. The more touch points you make, the bigger you play.

How many ways can you interact with customers and potential investors? The possibilities today are numerous and can influence people before, during, and after a purchase. Every touch point with a customer is an opportunity to improve the customer experience, develop and increase value for the customer, and gain customer commitment.

Some of us still remember the AT&T advertising campaign, "Reach out and touch someone." The message was simple: reach out and connect with a loved one, a family member, or a friend through AT&T long-distance telephone calls.

BOOM
THOUGHT 4.4

One of the best ways to Play Big is to be thoughtful and engaging. Reach out and touch as often and in as many ways as possible!

One way to think about customer touch points is to consider the customer's experience in buying and using a product. The process starts with the customer (1) recognizing a problem, need, or opportunity. Then the customer (2) searches for information about products that can solve the problem, address the need, or capitalize on the opportunity. The customer (3) evaluates the alternative solutions and then (4) makes a purchase decision. Finally, the customer (5) uses the product with an expectation that the product will deliver value by solving the problem, addressing the need, or capitalizing on the opportunity.

Think about how you can connect with customers during each stage of product search, purchase, and usage. As an example, car manufacturers learned years ago that more people went to their websites after purchasing one of their cars than before purchasing one of their cars. Smart manufacturers managed the touch point by highlighting testimonials from happy customers and spotlighting awards for initial purchase satisfaction and long-term quality.

We recommend using something like the planning table shown on the following page to list potential touch points for each stage of the customer experience and the specific activities you will establish and manage, such as face-to-face meeting, telephone conversation, email note, website content, trade publication, product literature, trade show, media-based advertising, service calls, customer visits, etc.

Managing Customer Touch Points

STEPS IN CUSTOMER EXPERIENCE	POTENTIAL CUSTOMER TOUCH POINTS
Problem recognition	
Information search	
Evaluation of alternatives	
Purchase	
Usage	
Post-purchase evaluation	

Do You Know the Determinants?

Research in service quality[8] suggests that regardless of the type of exchange, consumers use largely the same criteria in evaluating the quality of the experience. We think of each of these criteria as an opportunity to interject a number of touch points. The table below lists the 10 determinants of service quality.

1. Reliability	Perform promised service dependably and accurately
2. Responsiveness	Willingness and readiness to provide service
3. Competence	Possession of skills/knowledge to perform the service
4. Access	Approachability and ease of contact
5. Courtesy	Politeness, respect, consideration, and friendliness
6. Communication	Listen; keep customer informed
7. Credibility	Trust, believability, honesty, seeking customer's best interest
8. Security	Freedom from danger, risk, or doubt
9. Customer Knowledge	Understand the customer's needs
10. Tangibles	Appearance of physical facilities, equipment, personnel, etc.

Just think, at each touch point your customer may be evaluating your reliability, or your responsiveness, or your competence, or the access to you and your company, or your courtesy, or your communication, or your credibility, or the security in doing business with you, or your knowledge of their particular needs, or your tangible cues of success and stability, or a combination of the above or all of the above. Performing well on these criteria, by managing the touch points, provides an opportunity to gain or build commitment with the customer.

Make the Sale with Touch Points!

One of the most effective salespeople we've observed in an entrepreneurial business was a true master at finding and leveraging

[8]See "A Conceptual Model of Service Quality and Its Implications for Future Research," by A. Parasuraman, Valarie A. Zeithaml, and Leonard L. Berry, *Journal of Marketing* (Fall 1985), 41-50.

touch points. When you have a small business it is easy to be overlooked, but if you can't be big in size, you can be big in action. This salesperson reserved a couple of hours each day for calling potential clients, bringing them up-to-date on things happening in his company, getting up-to-date on things happening in their company, asking for new business, or at least asking for the opportunity to respond to a RFP or make a presentation.

This master of the touch point also clipped articles from newspapers and magazines that would be of interest to potential clients and mailed them off with a little note, sent relevant website links via email, gave away personalized calendars each year, and gifted small but unique Christmas mementos. Does the tactic work? He doubled the sales revenue of the next best salesperson.

What startups don't have in national reputation they can make up for by giving world-class personal attention. People buy from people they know. People buy from people they like. But most importantly, people buy from people they trust. Reaching out with touch points and then making each touch point personal and memorable builds trust. Smallness can empower startups to gain trust by doing things with real gusto that larger, more established companies wouldn't even consider.

Best Practice: Build a Spider Web

Most spiders build webs or cobwebs with the silk they produce from their three pairs of spinnerets. Spider silk is stronger than the equivalent weight of steel and much more elastic. With their webs, spiders catch food without having to chase their prey—more meals while expending less energy! Sometimes spiders even build their webs together to increase their efficiency in capturing prey. At Lake Tawakoni State Park in Texas, a group of stretch spiders once constructed a series of webs that measured over 200 yards.

We can learn a lot from the effectiveness and efficiencies of spider webs. A crucial part of a successful entrepreneurial venture is to use a "connected" advisory board to generate

BOOM
THOUGHT 4.5

Extend your influence by assembling an advisory board that is well-connected to the community and/or industry you want to enter.

or catch more business. An advisory board can extend your social network of influence to increase its effectiveness and efficiencies in attracting investors, customers, and top employees. No new venture is too small or too large to benefit from an advisory board. Leveraging advisory board experience, expertise, and connections is the best way to succeed in today's competitive markets.

Playing big requires a startup firm to have a national or regional reputation. Perhaps one of the best-kept secrets of successful entrepreneurial firms is they know that reputation and experience counts, and that it doesn't have to be their own. We can't emphasize enough what we stated earlier in SuperLaw #2—Ride Horses. Successful entrepreneurs know that **hard work**, i.e., working 100 hours a week, rarely leads to a successful new venture. It is the **smart work of yourself and others**, especially a credible and useful advisory board, that leads to new venture success.

We have observed, however, that many startup firms focus on developing their board of directors instead of beginning with an advisory board. Advisory boards have two key advantages over a board of directors:

1. Advisory boards often are not paid in equity or cash like formal boards. Thus advisory boards can be a low-cost and high-value alternative for startups.
2. Advisory board members can't be sued for their advice because they do not have any fiduciary responsibility to stockholders as do members of the board of directors. Thus, advisory boards are usually made up of nonpolitical, fun, and creative professionals who have a genuine interest and sincere desire to see you succeed.

Whenever you start a new venture, leverage the experience, wisdom, and creativity of advisory members to accelerate the growth of your new venture. Of course having a world-class advisory board does send the message that you play big.

Advisory board members should not be limited to businesspeople who have launched successful startups themselves or accomplished other things related to your new business. Also include people who possess local, regional, or national name recognition. For example, prominent politicians, retired executives or managers, and industry gurus make great advisory board members. Advice really is cheap and advisory board members can save you years of painful and costly mistakes. Advisory board members who are willing to use their own time, influence, and contacts to promote your company are truly priceless. Like horses, advisory board members are motivated to help you because they love to be associated with up-and-coming ventures. Minimal resources are needed to attract participation in an advisory board. Everyone loves a winner, and advisory board members are no exception. If perks like free lunches, dinners, or golf outings don't work, then attract advisory board members with a nominal 5,000 to 10,000 shares or options—assuming around 10,000,000 shares are presently outstanding.

Advisory boards help you play big by promoting a successful image for your company. Building a connected advisory network like the spider web is immeasurably more effective than creating your own social network from the ground up. Learn from the stretch spider and build your own series of social connections with a world-class advisory board to better capture your investors, customers, and key employees while expending less time, energy, and money. To bring this chapter full circle, please remember to surround yourself with reputable people, because that is playing big and being smart.

Review Questions

Define with Five

Define the following vocabulary words using five words or less.

1. Puffer Fish

_____

2. Mavens

_____

3. Rule of Three

_____

4. Touch Points

_____

5. Courtesy

_____

Question the Answer

Answer each phrase below in the form of a question.

1. Once this is lost among business partners and customers it is very difficult to repair.

_____

2. Not about lying, telling half-truths, bending agreements, or manipulating financials.

_____

3. Keeps your product focused and focuses buyers on key product benefits.

_____

4. It weighs 43 tons and fires a 2200-pound shell over nine miles.

_____

5. Inexpensively extends your social network and influence.

_____

Smarter than an Entrepreneur

Name the product or venture that reinforces or violates a Boom Start best practice.

1. Tapped into the power of the underdog even though they were a market leader.

_____

2. Embraced #2 when they realized it did more for their business than being #1.

_____

3. Learned the hard way that little amounts of mind share add up to little amounts of profit.

_____

4. The imaginative brand name for this dessert evokes strong feelings and emotions.

_____

5. Aggressively flaunts their underdog status when selling employee and customer engagement surveys and management feedback systems.

_____

SuperLaws in Action

A catchphrase focuses the business and focuses customers on the key product benefit. A great catchphrase will wrap your benefit in bacon while putting heat on your competitors' weaknesses. It works by throwing us into a quandary or by touching our emotions.

Activity: Be clever and invent catchphrases to capture our imagination for the three products described below:

Need: A big, enjoyable meal that satisfies

Product: Huge broiler-cooked burger of delicious beef

Catchphrase: _____

Need: A new flavor of toothpaste that tastes great and makes my mouth feel minty-fresh

Product: Mint vanilla toothpaste

Catchphrase: _____

Need: Makeup that accentuates natural beauty without looking fake

Product: Light makeup that doesn't look thick or clumpy

Catchphrase: _____

Do an Event

Great entrepreneurs are great at creating buzz and impact with limited funds. They create buzz not by aggressive advertising, renting billboards, or flooding the airwaves with radio spots, but by inventing and doing marketing events. Put your creative thinking cap on! Get experiential! Create memorable experiences that people can take home with them!

For years we have taught introductory marketing courses to many students at many different universities. Through all the differences from person to person and from school to school, there is one great constant. New marketing students seem to think every marketing problem can be solved either by doing more advertising or by charging a lower price. Successfully launch a new product—more advertising, lower price. Improve sales of a failing product—more advertising, lower price. Deflect the attack of a competitive product—more advertising, lower price. Build brand equity and accelerate repeat sales—more advertising, lower price.

Fighting in the trenches of a startup business, however, practicing marketers soon discover that high-cost advertising and price cuts are not the panaceas that novices seem to think they are. First and foremost, both are too expensive for cash-starved entrepreneurs. In the case of advertising, today's media channels are so fragmented it is difficult for advertisers to reach potential customers efficiently. Just spending a lot of money and reaching a lot of people doesn't add up to a lot of anything for most entrepreneurial products. A case in point: Super Bowl XXIV will be forever remembered more for the dot-com advertising excesses and failures than the two football teams that played. On that Sunday, a dozen or so Internet startups spent over $40 million to air a grand total of 10 minutes of advertisements. And that $40 million amount only covered the media buy. Millions more were spent to produce the spots. In spite of their large ad-spend, most of the startups were quickly dead and gone. The dot-com entrepreneurs apparently fell into the Marketing 101 mind trap, falsely believing that big advertising solves all the big marketing problems.

Just think about it. Did you see any television advertising last week? How many ads do you remember? Of those, how many advertisers do you remember? In modern America, it takes tens of millions, even hundreds of millions of dollars to burn an advertising message into the public consciousness. As marketers, we hate to admit it, but most paid advertising is often really, really ineffective. It is at its strongest when reassuring people about purchases they have already made or passing on some good news about awards, accomplishments, or fun events. It is at its weakest when attempting to persuade people to purchase new products.

If Not Advertising, Then What?

In 1970, Congress passed a law banning television and radio advertising of tobacco products. Congress believed that stopping advertising was the key to stopping teen smoking. They were thinking, "If we want to destroy new sales and cause product failure, squelch all advertising"—that same old Marketing 101 mind trap with a twist. Unfortunately, the advertising ban on tobacco hasn't worked out for Congress or the American people. According to the CDC, every day in the US, more than 3,000 young people become regular smokers. That adds up to more than a million new smokers a year. To add to that, teen smoking rates have increased each year for the last 10 years. Marketing 101 students are left to wonder, "How can the tobacco industry have all of this success without the powerful aid of television and radio advertising?"

Congress forced Big Tobacco away from Big Advertising to a much less expensive and much more effective marketing tactic—the marketing event. After the ban, it wasn't long before wildly successful marketing events like Marlboro Country Nights were attracting teens by the thousands to hear their favorite country-western acts and to learn from their friends the social benefits of smoking. Dreaming up a successful marketing event takes a lot more time, energy, and creativity then just handing over big bucks to a big-name advertising agency. But time, energy, and creativity are exactly what entrepreneurs have to offer. Entrepreneurs and marketing events appear to be a match made in marketing heaven.

As the costs to launch a new brand go up and up, even large companies are getting more entrepreneurial. In cooperation with the House of Blues, Honda Motors sponsored "Fit in the House" music concerts from San Diego, California to Atlantic City, New Jersey. As part of the event, a Fit Custom Art Car, painted by House of Blues folk artist Jack Poppitz, was auctioned off. Proceeds went to the House of Blues Foundation, which encourages music and art in schools and local communities. For each concert, the Fit was featured prominently in front of the House of Blues venue with colorful, brand-themed lanterns posted on either side of the vehicle. Honda took the vehicle directly to the young, hip crowd they believed were most likely to buy it. Potential customers saw the car, sat in the car, and learned that the Fit was hip.

Even television shows have found that they need to use something in addition to traditional television advertising to promote their programming. On the day of the premiere of VH1's "I Love the 90s," over 50 models danced through the streets of Manhattan dressed like 90s celebrities such as Bill Clinton, Monica Lewinsky, MC Hammer, Pamela Anderson, and other crowd-pleasers. The look-alikes did the Macarena in high-traffic areas including Times Square and Grand Central Station, giving away stickers encouraging everyone to tune in for VH1's new 90s series.

In recent years we also have seen television producers and sponsors embed marketing events into television programs as part of the storyline to generate interest in the program as well as new products. Procter & Gamble achieved the highest online interest in a new product launch in their history when they sponsored an episode of the reality TV program *The Apprentice*. The episode featured two teams of businesspeople competing to stage the best marketing event to launch a new flavor of Crest toothpaste: mint vanilla. Building on the idea, program viewers were encouraged to enter an essay contest to describe in 100 words or less how they would have promoted the new toothpaste flavor. The P&G website received 100 essays a minute in the first 20 minutes after the show ended. In total, over 20,000 applicants participated in the contest. The website received over 4.7 million product-related hits and 40,000 samples of mint vanilla Crest were requested.

Entrepreneurial companies also have run across some great ideas for marketing events. In many ways, entrepreneurs have more freedom than large companies to do something unique and creative. A local roller coaster designer and amusement ride manufacturer sent their marketing director out on a road trip to amusement parks across the country driving a VW Bug he personally purchased and modified to mimic the look and feel of the amusement park ride he was promoting. The event stirred up a lot of interest among park patrons, which in turn sparked interest in the new ride from park operators and owners.

Best Practice: Get Experiential

As good as the ideas of these marketing events are, entrepreneurs can still do better. When compared to their corporate counterparts, entrepreneurs often fight a much tougher battle for the minds and hearts of customers. To meet that challenge, entrepreneurs need to push beyond staging a marketing event to creating personalized marketing experiences. A personalized marketing experience enables customers to gain firsthand experience with a product while at the same time providing an opportunity for the customer to take some of the product experience home to act as a daily reminder. Amusement parks figured this out decades ago. We love to ride the big roller coaster: the one that drops straight down and then turns multiple loops upside down. It is thrilling, and like us, most people want to take some of the thrill home. Knowing this, amusement parks set up small souvenir stands to sell hats and shirts and other small items highlighting the roller coaster experience. Sometimes you can even pick up a picture of yourself laughing, cheering, or screaming during the ride itself.

> ## BOOM
> ──────THOUGHT 5.1──────
>
> *To make an event experiential, first create an exciting hands-on activity with the product, and then provide a free souvenir that brings the excitement home.*

Creating a personalized marketing experience is very similar to creating a successful roller coaster ride. First there is the ride, and then there is the personalized souvenir. More specifically, first create an interesting, even thrilling firsthand experience with the product. Second, provide a small item as a souvenir the participant can take home that personalizes the experience.

For an example of the "Step One, Step Two" event planning process, consider the experiential marketing event orchestrated by Polaroid and Jelly Belly Candy Company. Several years ago, Jelly Belly launched a national road tour. As the tour visited popular shopping and other high-traffic areas throughout the US, consumers sampled old and new flavors of Jelly Belly jelly beans. Next, personalized photos of family and friends were shot using Polaroid film with a pre-exposed border featuring the Jelly Belly logo. The souvenir and the happy memories of the Jelly Belly tasting experience then returned home to be posted on the kitchen refrigerator. In total, about 20,000 free photos went home during the 150-city tour, increasing top-of-mind awareness and brand loyalty, and making sweet increases in Jelly Belly sales.

How to Construct a Winning Marketing Event

Every year, *Promo Magazine* recognizes the best of the best promotions and marketing events. Several years ago, Cadillac won the top award for its "Cadillac Under 5" promotion, in which contestants made five-second films to spotlight the new car's power. The contest drew 2,648 entries, drove site traffic up by 358% with one million new visitors, and delivered nearly 45,000 incremental requests for dealer information.

As we look over the winners from year to year, we look for recurring themes. What does it take to make a winner? Below we list five "secret sauce" rules for dreaming up successful promotions and marketing events.

Rule #1: Make sure the distinctive product feature takes center stage in the event.

From what we've observed, promotions are judged on short-term results, but goodness is also judged on strategic impact. For example, the *Promo Magazine* judges particularly liked that the "Cadillac Under 5" promotion directly sold the premise of the car. The power and speed of the vehicle took center stage in creating excitement and were not peripheral to the event.

Rule #2: Make it gorgeous; event quality reflects on product quality.

HP is another award winner with the "You + HP Experience" interactive tour. It consisted of a modular structure moved from town to town like a traveling high-tech circus spotlighting over 40 products via 12 interactive concourses. Consumers photographed themselves using pop-culture backdrops, printed pictures with HP gear, and watched videos using HP digital projectors and plasma TVs. The tour attracted about one million visitors at 45 events spread across the US and Canada. The judges were impressed with the professional execution and how "gorgeous" the concourses and activities looked.

Rule #3: If at all possible, connect the event with a local cause.

Events that promote a product and a popular local cause are also frequent winners. Washington Mutual used a bus to tour Los Angeles and Seattle schools to encourage parents to support their WaMoola program. WaMoola is money donated to support local schools donated from each Washington Mutual check-card transaction. Card applications jumped and card use increased by 42%.

Rule #4: Target the event to fit a specific audience and marketing objective.

Another key to a successful event is careful targeting. Gatorade is an award winner for its "Gatorade High School Athlete Award Program." In this promotion, high school coaches registered for an awards kit to honor their top athletes. The judges were impressed because it was simple for the coaches, but more importantly because it "targeted coaches by sport, by boys or girls, and by past participation." Gatorade's targeted approach achieved a 30% response rate with over 50% of the active coaches re-enrolling.

Rule #5: Send home a personalized souvenir to drive home the brand experience.

Finally, we want to return to the Jelly Belly candy promotion. Judges were very impressed with the Jelly Belly logo photo that allowed consumers to take something home even though the product itself was consumed. The Jelly Belly eating experience doesn't leave anything other than some pleasant memories. The souvenir put a personalized, long-term Jelly Belly reminder in the home.

Best Practice: Have a Love Fest

If you want new customers to feel the excitement of your new product, let your customers sell it for you. Sponsor your own events and generate Love Fest buzz. Putting together a successful Love Fest is a two-step process. Step One: Create opportunities for your best customers to "share the love" they have for your products and services. Step Two: Get out of the way and let your customers sell for you.

New startups need to orchestrate ways for their evangelists to spread the message of love—that is, the good news about their favorite company and products. The ultimate high-credibility information source is customer talking to customer or customer talking to new prospect. A Love Fest leverages "customer love" so that current customers buy more from you and pre-sell more of your products to new customers.

So, how do you create these Love Fests among your customers and prospective customers? The answer is any way you can imagine. Love Fests can be leading-edge conferences, summits, events, blogs, clubs, community classes, or any other activities that bring your current customers and prospective customers together. The goal is to get your customers together, in person or in virtual space, to learn, share, enjoy, and celebrate their personal connections to your company and products.

H.O.G. Means L.O.V.E.

Owner groups provide a forum for customers to exchange ideas and educate each other about the important benefits of product ownership as well as product uses, usage situations, and complementary products. The idea is to get customers celebrating the brand together. This Love Fest of owners creates increased interest in the product, generates useful ideas for the company, earns more

© Reuters/CORBIS

Harley-Davidson Rules

The Harley Owners Group may be the world's single best example of how a brand can successfully connect with brand lovers. It bridges the gap between all types of riders and enthusiasts. It provides almost endless opportunities for growth through line and brand extensions.

sales from customers, and promotes interest and sales among non-customers.

As an example, let's consider the Harley Owners Group, aka H.O.G. Who has more love than H.O.G. members? In 1983, Harley-Davidson formed H.O.G. "to enhance the Harley-Davidson lifestyle experience, and to bring the company closer to its customers."[1] And bring customers together, in a Love Fest way, they did. Today more than a million people around the world pride themselves as H.O.G. members. Wouldn't you love to have a million customers selling for you? And what do they sell? They sell the Harley-Davidson dream and making it a way of life. Could you ask for more? One million Harley-Davidson owners, selling their friends, neighbors, and relatives on the Harley-Davidson dream. And they sell themselves on group events such as rides, open houses, pin stops, pit stops, and of course, products. "The annual value of an active H.O.G. member is estimated at $5,575, while even inactive members are valued at $4,725."[2] Membership is a roaring success for Harley-Davidson.

An Apple a Day

For Apple lovers, users, and all-out devotees, Macworld hosts the ultimate Love Fest with expos, conferences, trade shows, a maga-

---

[1] *Building Brand Community on the Harley-Davidson Posse Ride*, by Susan Fourmier (Boston, Harvard Business School, 2000)
[2] Ibid.

zine, and a website. If you want to celebrate everything Apple, Macworld provides the venues. This shared love for Apple generates significant buzz among Apple's brand champions. Many of them become so connected to the brand they begin to act like latter-day evangelists, preaching the good news about Apple to their co-workers, friends, and each other.

The Apple Love Fest represents a significant force in Apple's marketing efforts. Imagine having thousands of Love Group customers extolling the virtues of your product to the market and selling your product. And this is highly effective and highly efficient voice-of-the-customer selling, not megabuck paid advertising available to only deep-pocket corporations.

Creating Memorable Events

Love Fest events can energize existing customers and provide significant visibility in front of prospective customers. Omniture, a market leader in online business optimization software, discovered the value of creating Love Fest events early in its history.

Together with his colleagues, Omniture CEO and co-founder Josh James created a memorable event at an e-tailing trade show. The company sponsored a lunch for all conference participants. The goal, according to Josh, was to get every person at the conference to know and remember Omniture. But it takes more than a trade-show lunch to create a memorable event. So, Omniture teamed with one of its customers, General Motors, to give away a one-year lease for a new Hummer to a lucky trade show participant. Imagine the excitement this created.

The event included a multi-round rock-paper-scissors competition. However, Josh made one simple, yet significant, change in the game. Instead of saying "One, two, three," or "Rock, paper, scissors," participants yelled, "Om, ni, ture!" So, during lunch, Ominiture first invited everyone to stand up, and then asked its competitors to sit down. While competitors could only sit and watch, all those standing played the game, each time chanting the name, "Om, ni, ture!" Soon the large dining hall was rocking with the sound "Om, ni, ture!" Toy Hummers were given away at each table for elimination winners in the early rounds. Each table advanced a winner to the next round. Finally, two were left standing for the final round. And, with each round, with each play, the entire hall yelled "Om, ni, ture" until the winner was declared. Customers were energized. Prospective customers were curious. They wanted to know more about this company, Omniture. To this date, if you ask a participant at that trade show what was the one most memorable event, the immediate answer is, "Om, ni, ture."

Classes, Blogs, and Contests

Only several years ago, Lance Anderson started Rusty Pickle, a creator and provider of papers, binders, stickers, die cuts, transparencies, albums, ribbons, and other materials for scrapbook companies and scrapbook enthusiasts. The company tagline is "Adding texture and dimension to scrapbooking!" But this is not all. The company also adds texture and dimension to retail stores and customers by providing classes, contests, and even a blog.

Teaching scrapbook classes at retailers and shows coast to coast is a core activity for Rusty Pickle. Almost weekly, the company representatives are on the road teaching scrapbook aficionados, experts, and beginners the art and love of scrapbooking. Of course, retailers love these classes because they generate a Love Fest buzz about scrapbooks, which means more sales for the retailer. And customers love sharing ideas and learning about new products with other experts as well as with beginners. The Love Fest buzz then takes on a life outside the classes as customers show off their newly acquired scrapbooking skills to family and friends.

And then there is the Rusty Pickle blog. This virtual venue creates a Love Fest forum for customers and scrapbook junkies to learn and to share the love of scrapbooking. Here are just a few voice-of-the-customer comments from the Rusty Pickle blog:

> *You guys have the best things!!!*

> *WOW!! WOW!! WOW!! Another acrylic album. What does a girl have to do to get her hands on one of those?????!!!! I started to put together one of your kits the other night and oh my, so fun! I can't wait to get some of this great new stuff!*

> *Simply . . . I *heart* Rusty Pickle! :)*

> *I was recently introduced to Rusty Pickle by Libby M! I am drooling over the Picklicious Line!!!*

Can you feel the love? Wouldn't you love to have a Libby M. introduce your products to new customers? For startups willing to trust the love, a Love Fest offers up a powerful marketing juggernaut.

Clubs, the Ultimate Love Fests

Are you a connoisseur of fine chocolate, microbrews, power ties, or taste-kicking hot sauce? If so, you will want to join an online club where experts send you the newest product every month! A uniquely fun and effective Love Fest used by entrepreneurs is to start a club or community where product users can be united with a common set of interests and focus.

Entrepreneurs that organize clubs find an easy way to generate continuing revenue. Love Group customers are eager to participate in automatic monthly purchases just to be the first to try and comment on the latest and greatest flavor, color, or product improvement. Some people, for example, those buying ties, don't want to bother taking the time and energy to go to a retail store and shop on their own. Why not let *tie experts* pick out the *power tie of the month* and send it directly to you? Customers who join clubs love to share their knowledge and expertise with anyone who will read or listen. Make it happen for your product and organize a club for your customer community!

> ## BOOM
> ---THOUGHT 5.2---
> *Join the club of successful entrepreneurs by organizing a club for your customers to join. Offer them products of the month and an opportunity to be a product guru.*

Best Practice: Make Demonstrations Compelling

Product demonstrations generate a lot of energy and interest. Use demonstrations to show functionality and immediate results.

Thomas Edison is one of the all-time greatest entrepreneurs. Edison invented the light bulb, right? Actually, wrong: Edison did not invent the light bulb, but was the first to successfully commercialize the light bulb. He borrowed and improved upon the ideas of at least a couple of good neighbors—the scientist Humphry Davy, who made the first light bulb in 1800, and the physicist Sir Joseph Wilson Swan, who in 1860 invented the carbon filament. To successfully commercialize the light bulb, Edison bought the patents from its inventors, discovered how to make a bulb burn for more than 1,500 hours, and then discovered how to get people excited about it.

Edison was an expert at making compelling product demonstrations. On New Year's Eve, he arranged for a public demonstration of his incandescent lights. Interested and influential spectators arrived on special trains from New York City to view the Menlo Park laboratory, grounds, and an adjacent boarding house glowing with 100 electric light bulbs.

After conquering the light bulb, Edison marched forward to fight the electricity war to decide whether direct current (DC) electricity or alternating current (AC) electricity would be used in our homes and businesses. Edison represented DC and his rival Nikola Tesla, with the financial backing of George Westinghouse, represented AC. Edison believed his best chance to win the electricity war was to convince the public that AC was too dangerous to have in their homes. His main weapon in the fight was making public demonstrations of AC's lethal power. An Edison employee staged several events for reporters in which dogs and cats were "Westinghoused" to death with AC electricity. The biggest demonstration, however, was the electrocution of the ill-tempered, man-killing Coney Island elephant Topsy, which was witnessed by more than 1,500 reporters and interested bystanders.

> # BOOM
> ### THOUGHT 5.3
> *An old proverb says, "Hear it and I forget it. See it and I remember it. Do it and I understand it." Demonstrate the positive consequences of using a product so people can see it, touch it, and understand it.*

The papers reported that cyanide couldn't kill the elephant, but Westinghouse electricity could. Edison also maneuvered to have AC used in the first electric chairs and released his own film to the movie houses of the day entitled *Electrocution of Czolgosz*; a detailed reenactment of the electrocution of President McKinley's assassin. The film shows the prison the morning of the execution, the corridor leading up to murderer's row, Czolgosz walking to the death chamber as the final tests of the electric chair are being made, Czolgosz being strapped to the chair, his body violently jerking as the electricity passes through his body, and finally, the coroner pronouncing him dead.

Edison's demonstrations were so successful that Tesla, determined not to be beat, was forced into making a daring demonstration of his own. In addition to charging one-half of what Edison asked for lighting the Chicago Exposition of 1893, Tesla invited the public and reporters to watch as he gripped wires in his hands and let AC electricity pass through his body to power a light bulb. One good demonstration deserves another. In the end, Tesla lost a few battles, but ultimately won the war because of his daring demonstration and the fact that his brand of electricity was the most practical to transport over long distances. Even Edison later admitted that from the beginning he knew that AC electricity was the best.

Not All Product Demonstrations Are Equally Good

Seeing is believing! When people see it, they can understand it! Product demonstrations work and should be part of every entrepreneur's toolkit. We are not talking about simple variants of food sampling that everyone sees in grocery stores. We are referring to full-out demonstrations of even pricey items in which people have a chance to handle the product and experience its benefits firsthand.

We have said this before, but it bears repeating. People want proof, not puffery, and this is particularly true for startups and entrepreneurs. Generations of fast-talking salespeople and over-the-top advertising have made the public skeptical of product claims,

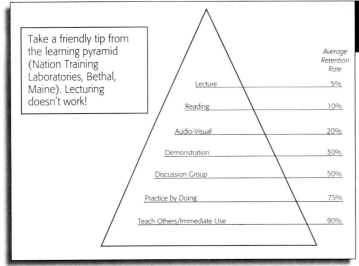

Take a friendly tip from the learning pyramid (Nation Training Laboratories, Bethal, Maine). Lecturing doesn't work!

	Average Retention Rate
Lecture	5%
Reading	10%
Audio-Visual	20%
Demonstration	30%
Discussion Group	50%
Practice by Doing	75%
Teach Others/Immediate Use	90%

Often Demonstrations Are Little More Than Lectures

Effective demonstrations require a lot of thought, planning, and preparation. Demonstrations need to engage people with something active. Product lectures are forgettable and do little to promote a new product.

and each new generation seems to be more skeptical than the last. Growing skepticism and boredom with sales pitches unfortunately means that not all demonstrations will be equally good. In today's world, demonstrations almost always must be active in order to be effective. There is a big difference between active and passive demonstrations. Passive demonstrations are like lectures. Just take a look at the learning pyramid shown above to see how effective lectures are!

Active demonstrations get people doing rather than just watching. Active demonstrations give people hands-on experience. Great demonstrations are just like great games: everyone wants a chance to play. Developing a great game takes some creativity and ingenuity, but not great sums of money.

DuPont Stainmaster developed one of the best demonstration games of recent history. Consumers walking into carpet stores were led by retailers to a kiosk where they could soak light-colored swatches of Stainmaster carpet in their favorite stains, then wash out the stain completely in seconds using a simple solution of soap and water. If you've never seen it, believe us when we say it is a very convincing demonstration. Upon its introduction, Stainmaster became the sales leader and is still the reigning carpet sales champion. The phenomenal commercial success of Stainmaster resulted from a carefully orchestrated plan of product innovation, branding, performance guarantee, memorable advertising, and learn-by-doing demonstration. Every part of the program was important, but product insiders will tell you that the demonstration kiosk was key for making product sales.

What Demonstrations Should Demonstrate

Effective demonstrations do a lot more than just demonstrate what the product does. In the case of Stainmaster, the demonstration showed off the carpet's "relative advantage" over other carpets. Relative advantage, however, is something that goes above and beyond a product benefit.

Is this starting to sound complicated? It isn't really. It turns out that there is a theory about all of this. Just as a reminder, Everett Rogers researched the spread of new ideas and products through society.[3] In his research he identified five kinds of people he called

---

[3] *Diffusion of Innovations,* by Everett Rogers (1995)

innovators, early adopters, early majority, late majority, and laggards. Depending on the sort of person you are, you will be more or less likely to be the first on your block to buy a new, innovative product.

His research also identified five things that will speed everyone, even laggards, to more readily adopt new products. These are "relative advantage," "compatibility," "complexity," "trialability," and "observability." When developing an active demonstration, we want to hit as many of these quick-acceptance touchstones as possible. Relative advantage means the new product is much better than the old product it replaces. Compatibility means that the new product fits in with the typical way we go about doing things. Humans are creatures of habit. Demonstrations should show that people don't need to radically change their day-to-day behaviors to get the most out of a new product. Complexity really should be called anti-complexity, because it is the degree to which a new product is easy for people to understand and use. Trialability refers to how accessible a product is for hands-on trial and experimentation. Observability is the degree to which we can observe others using and enjoying the new product.

With these concepts in hand, it is interesting to review the Stainmaster experience. The Stainmaster kiosk was set up to highlight relative advantage by providing red cough syrup as the benchmark stain. Carpet buyers knew a tough stain when they saw it, and they knew how impossible it would be to remove from their own carpeting. With Stainmaster, the red syrup stain washed clean again and again using only simple soap and water. No need for fancy cleaners, processes, or chemicals; nothing could be simpler than soap and water. The Stainmaster in-store demonstration encompassed relative advantage, compatibility, anti-complexity, and trialability. One could even say that the DuPont kiosk incorporated observability when interested carpet buyers watched as others stained then washed bits of Stainmaster before taking their own turn! One can only imagine as the next buyer in line would walk up to the kiosk and try twice as hard as the previous customer to stain the carpet, and the look of shock and excitement when they couldn't.

BOOM

THOUGHT 5.4

Energize your product demonstrations by incorporating the elements leading to speedy product adoption, especially relative advantage, compatibility, and trialability.

DuPont could have taken a different approach to product demonstration. Instead of providing a kiosk demonstration center, company managers could have asked retailers to hand out samples of Stainmaster and a set of instructions for prospective carpet buyers to take home and try out on their own. While much cheaper and perhaps easier to implement, this approach would have been a lot less fun and dramatic, virtually eliminated observability, made it more difficult to control relative advantage, increased the complexity for the buyer, and removed the demonstration from the point of purchase.

The Big Three: Relative Advantage, Compatibility, Trialability

Not every product demonstration can bring together each element identified by Everett Rogers in his book about diffusion of innovation. For entrepreneurs there are, however, three must-haves to include. Research shows that, in general, relative advantage and compatibility are the two most important factors energizing new product diffusion. Looking at years of data spanning dozens of industries and product categories, it is clear that success often comes to those new products that are superior to their predecessors and mesh with rather than interrupt our way of life. If you are an entrepreneur and have one of those products, use a demonstration to highlight the fact.

Finally, because we know doing is more powerful than watching, we also recommend that every demonstration include an element of hands-on trialability. If you own a camera shop and sell digital cameras, let people take a few pictures of the salespeople and experience the technological miracle for themselves. If you invent a product to keep hands dry, take it to a golf course on a hot and humid day and let golfers experience how much better they can hold on to their slippery grips. The possibilities are endless. Just make sure that after making your fantastic demonstration you give people an opportunity to buy, because they will want to, and you can't let that special moment pass!

Review Questions

Define with Five

Define the following vocabulary words using five words or less.

1. Marketing Event

_____

2. Love Fest

_____

3. Active Demonstration

_____

4. Marketing Experience

_____

5. Complexity

_____

Question the Answer

Answer each phrase below in the form of a question.

1. These "go to" marketing tactics are usually too expensive for cash-starved startups.

_____

2. Enables customers to gain firsthand experience with a product as well as to take some of the product home as a daily reminder.

_____

3. Stress distinctive features, make it gorgeous, connect with local causes, target a specific audience, send home a souvenir.

_____

4. Usually forgettable and do little to successfully promote a new product.

_____

5. It is at its weakest when trying to persuade people to purchase new products.

_____

Smarter than an Entrepreneur

Name the product or venture that reinforces or violates a Boom Start best practice.

1. Co-sponsored events with the House of Blues to successfully promote a new car launch.

_____

2. Discovered that marketing events are more powerful than advertising when Congress forced their promotional messages off the airwaves.

_____

3. Teamed up for sweet success using the "Step One, Step Two" event planning process.

_____

4. One of the first American businesses to leverage the power of the Love Fest.

_____

5. Gained national attention when spending $5 million for less than two minutes of Super Bowl advertising, just to go out of business almost as quickly.

_____

5 SuperLaws in Action

Marketing events, particularly when they are intellectually and emotionally engaging, are powerful tools for cash-starved startups. Mastering marketing events will take the entrepreneur a long way towards building a successful business.

Activity: Create a marketing event to nourish the bottom line of Ralph's Supermarkets by getting local elementary school children excited about eating healthful food and parents excited about buying it for them.

Describe the event by making a "point of sale" poster for placement in Ralph's that announces the event:

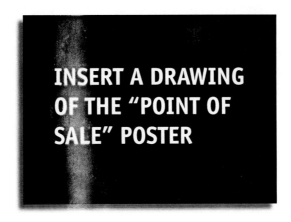

The event will get kids excited to eat healthful foods because . . .

The event will get parents excited about buying healthful foods for their kids because . . .

chapter 6 Reap the Rewards

Perfect products don't guarantee entrepreneurial success. Combining a good product with a sharp angle directed at a high-value opportunity is more important than finding absolute perfection out of the starting gate. So don't wait for the perfect product: start reaping the rewards of your effort as soon as possible. Most people are surprisingly forgiving when a fresh idea with real merit hits the marketplace.

Everyone in a new business must know how to sell, close, and start reaping the benefits of their great ideas and entrepreneurial energy! Good entrepreneurs must be great at selling and making the most of what the market will give.

Best Practice: Be a Closer

The first step toward "reaping" is learning how to close! Experiment with different selling tactics and find the closer. When major league baseball managers need pitchers to save or finish a close game, they call on their ace closers like Mariano Rivera, Jonathan Papelbon, or Trevor Hoffman. These great closers, along with their counterparts on other major league baseball teams, play a significant role in their teams' success. They appear almost exclusively when the game is on the line. Their job is to save or "close" the game by getting the final outs. A key statistic for closers, which became official in 1969, is the number of saves. Another way to evaluate a closer's performance is to consider blown saves or the percentages of successful save opportunities. The great closers in baseball history—Dennis Eckersley, Rich "Goose" Gossage, Rollie

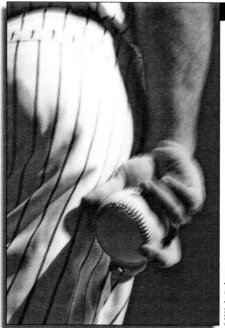

Learn to Sell—Learn to Close

It takes a great closer to reap the rewards of a great idea. Learning to ask "what if" questions, doing your homework on customer needs, knowing your "deal," and confidently asking for the sale are key components for successful closing.

© 2009. JupiterImages

Fingers, Lee Smith, Bruce Sutter—performed well on each of these statistics. Any way you look at it, great closers help their teams win games because they can finish games successfully.

Similarly, the role of closer is critical to the success of a new venture because the closer wins business for the company. Students and budding entrepreneurs often ask us, "What makes an entrepreneur successful?" Of course, the two textbook answers are (1) "It depends" and (2) "There are multiple determinants of success for entrepreneurs." While one may point out that this book is certainly evidence of the multiple determinants argument, there is, however, a secret: a secret that successful entrepreneurs understand well. And here is the secret: **successful entrepreneurs know how to sell and how to close!**

That's it. They know how to sell. They can finish the business. They can close the deal. And if they don't know how to sell, finish, and close, they quickly learn or at least find someone who can.

Although all functional areas of the entrepreneurial venture are important and necessary, selling plays the key role in getting and keeping investors and customers.

Avoid the Build-a-Better-Mousetrap Trap

Ralph Waldo Emerson said, "Build a better mousetrap and the world will beat a path to your door." This statement is true *if* the world knows that you sell mousetraps, *if* the world knows where to find your door, *if* the world understands the unique benefits of your mousetraps, and *if* the world knows how your mousetraps solve their mice problems better than alternative solutions and at a price they are willing to pay. Without this information, knowledge, and understanding, the beaten path will miss your door completely. Unfortunately, some entrepreneurs become so focused on "building the better mousetrap" that they do not spend enough effort or resources on selling it. Selling answers the above "*if*" statements. Don't ignore this important function along your way to building the better mousetrap. If you are to cash in on the rewards for developing a fantastic product, you must learn to close sales!

Harvard Business School Says Sell!

An interesting study by the Harvard Business School in 1996[1] examined the determinants of success for entrepreneurs. The sample included 87 Harvard Business School entrepreneurs and 100 entrepreneurs from the list of "Inc. 500" companies. One of the key findings from the study and recommendations to entrepreneurs is *learn to sell!*

> *"The data suggest that face-to-face selling is a crucial skill: for most ventures to have any chance of success the entrepreneur has to be able to call on a customer and secure an order for a product or service."*

Calling on a customer and securing an order means selling. It means asking the right questions and listening to customers to understand their needs and wants. It means matching the benefits of your product offering to the needs and wants of the customer. It means getting commitment from the customer for the order—that is, closing the deal. It means delivering on the commitments you make. It means meeting, even exceeding, customer expectations.

---

[1] *The Road Well Traveled*, by Amar Bhide (Harvard Business School Press, April 12, 1996)

Successful entrepreneurs know how to sell. They know how to close.

But selling for entrepreneurs is not without challenges. The Harvard research uncovered a number of selling challenges worth noting. We list the top three along with our recommended solutions:

Challenge 1

Entrepreneurs lack credibility—name recognition and track record. For example, they don't have the entrée that an IBM sales representative has with an MIS department. Also, prospects are likely to ask the question, "How do we know you are going to be around tomorrow?" In short, there is little or no trust.

Solution

Gain credibility; establish trust. One historically flawed sales assumption is that people buy from those they like. They don't. People buy from those they trust. To test this, simply look at your own experience. How many overly friendly salespeople have you found you could trust? To build a customer base over time, a business must establish trust with its customers, who must believe the business will meet or exceed their expectations. If customers' expectations are met or exceeded, the business grows. On the other hand, if customers' expectations are violated, the business dies.

Miller and Heiman[2] suggest that credibility and trust can be established by reputation, it can be transferred to you, and it can be earned by you. Establishing credibility by reputation is difficult for entrepreneurs because they have no track record.

Temporary credibility can be transferred to you by someone else recommending you, such as an introduction, a phone call, or an email. The person recommending you can be anyone the customer trusts: respected colleagues, business associates, friends, relatives, etc. You can draw on this transferred credibility until you earn your own.

Of course, the best way to gain credibility is to earn it yourself. Credibility is earned or lost with every interaction you have with a customer. Here are seven things you can do to earn credibility and trust with customers:

---

[2]Miller Heiman, Inc. (1997)

1. **Dress the part.** An old Scottish proverb counsels, "What e'er thou art, act well thy part." The first step in acting the part is dressing the part. People judge you by your appearance. Learn the business dress of your customers. When in doubt, err on the side of dressing up. Remember, you can always dress down, but you can't dress up.

2. **Speak the language of the customer.** Speak in terms the customer understands. Often sellers become so enamored with the exciting features of their products that they forget that customers do not buy features, they buy benefits. Think of the times you've suffered through a salesperson's laundry list of features not knowing why these features should be important to you. Theodore Levitt, Harvard Business School professor, said it well: "People don't want to buy a quarter-inch *drill*. They want a quarter-inch *hole*."[3] So, speak in terms of the hole (benefits), not the drill (features). If you do mention a feature, make sure you translate it into a benefit.

3. **Seek to understand.** Your primary task is to understand customers' problems and opportunities so that you can match what you have to offer with their needs and wants. Selling is not about you or about your company. It is about the customer. In the end, you want the customer to sell him/herself. Most people love to buy, but they do not like being sold to. So, help the customer buy. Ask good questions to help the customer uncover problems and opportunities.

4. **Listen, listen, listen.** Selling is not a standup monologue or a dog-and-pony show. It is a conversation, a dialogue—two people speaking. And who should speak more, the buyer or the seller? If the seller's objective is to "seek to understand," then the buyer should talk more. The seller can encourage the buyer to talk by asking good questions and by listening attentively.

5. **Set correct expectations.** Much of selling is managing customers' expectations. Don't promise the moon, unless you are committed to delivering it! Under-promise and over-deliver. Think about the times you've waited for a table at a restaurant. When the host/hostess tells you the wait is 15 minutes and then seats you in 10 minutes, you are thrilled. But when the host/hostess tells you the wait is 15 minutes and seats you in

---

[3] *The Innovator's Solution*, by Clayton M. Christensen and Michael E. Raynor (Boston, Harvard Business School Press, 2003), p. 99

20 minutes, you grumble all the way to the table. Manage customers' expectations. Under-promise and over-deliver.

6. **Be responsive.** A comparative advantage entrepreneurs have over larger Fortune 500 companies is the ability and willingness to respond quickly to customer requests. Tom Peters advocates "shocking levels of responsiveness, doing things in minutes and hours, which people did in weeks and months."[4]

7. **Deliver results.** In the final analysis, it is all about delivering results. Customers judge the performance of your company and products by how well you deliver on expectations. If you meet or exceed customers' expectations, they are likely to buy from you again and they may tell others about you. Conversely, if you don't meet their expectations, they certainly won't buy from you again and they will tell everyone they meet about you.

Challenge 2

Power is with the buyer. Entrepreneurs are in a weak selling position, particularly when their products represent discretionary purchases and their offerings lack distinctiveness.

Solution

Sell the angle. Your product and/or service must stand for something different that is important to the customers. The Harvard study is correct. If your product offering lacks distinctiveness, customers have no reason to try it.

Use the "so what" test to assess the importance and value customers place on your product offering. First, list each distinctive benefit of your product offering. How is it different from the competition? Then put yourself in the customers' shoes and ask, "So what?" "So what does this mean to me and my company?" "How does this relate to my problem?" "More importantly, how does this provide a solution to my problem?" Finally, provide a reason for customers to believe you can deliver on your promises. If you can't answer the "so what?" question or provide a "reason to believe" you can deliver, customers will pass on your product.

---

[4] *Power of Excellence* (video), by Tom Peters

DISTINCTIVE BENEFITS	SO WHAT?	REASONS TO BELIEVE

Challenge 3

Entrepreneurs must learn to subjugate their egos and deal with frequent rejection.

Solution

Check your ego at the customer's door. This is not the time to win debating points. Sure, you could win the battle of words, but you will lose the sale. This is a real test for many entrepreneurs who want to show how smart they are and who want to defend their product. Remember, the focus is not on you. The focus is on the customer.

A few years ago we conducted focus group interviews for an entrepreneur's new product. Regrettably, we invited the entrepreneur to sit in on the first focus group interview. This was a big mistake, because each time a member of the focus group questioned the product or made a negative comment about the product, the entrepreneur jumped to the product's defense. He was in "fight mode." He could not bear to hear a disparaging word about his new product without providing a counter-punch. Needless to say, we did not invite him to the next set of interviews.

Rejection is part of the entrepreneur's life. Not all customers will fall in love with your products. A big part of being a successful entrepreneur is learning how to cope with rejection. Our experience suggests that successful entrepreneurs use rejection as an opportunity to learn. They think hard about what steps to take to overcome future problems.

DIY or Outsource?

A major decision you must make is whether to sell the product yourself or look for partners to sell for you. Of course, if you cannot sell, if you are not willing to learn, and if you cannot find someone to teach you, then you should consider an outsource partner. Moreover, there are other strategic and cost reasons to consider.

First, let's consider the advantages of partners. Partners can provide instant access to customers. Dentrix Dental Systems found that value-added resellers (VARs) already had a presence in dental offices. By partnering with VARs, Dentrix received instant access to hundreds of dentists. More importantly, the VARs transferred credibility and trust to Dentrix.

By using partners, entrepreneurs save the cost of building and maintaining their own sales force. We have a friend in Eugene, Oregon who makes wood kits, such as clocks, birdhouses, home decorations, etc. for craft stores. He did not have the resources to build and maintain his own sales force, so he attended trade shows seeking partners to sell for him. He found a number of independent salespeople who sell to craft stores. They were eager to carry his line of wood kits. The good news for our entrepreneur friend is that he received instant access to hundreds of craft stores and he pays these independent salespeople only when they sell.

On the other hand, the major disadvantages of outsourcing the sales function are loss of control and loss of power.[5] When you outsource, you don't control the selling activity. You have little power over the salespeople who are selling your product. In addition, the selling partner develops and owns customer relationships. So, evaluate the strategic and cost considerations of "do it yourself" and "outsource." Which option can better sell, get the business, and close the deal for you?

Remember What Works

Customers buy your products and services for their own reasons. Take careful notes. Learn their hot buttons. What works for one

---

[5]"Match Your Sales Force Structure to Your Business Life Cycle," by Andris A. Zoltners, Prabhakant Sinha, and Sally E. Lorimer, in *Harvard Business Review* (July–August 2006), p. 82.

customer may work for another customer. Just like baseball closers remember which pitches work to finish games, you should remember what works in certain selling situations to close the deal. Then use this knowledge in similar selling situations.

Use the Summary-of-Benefits Close

Too many people think closing the sale is about using gimmicks and trick questions to get the customer to buy. This may work once, and only once. Remember the adage, "Fool me once, shame on you; fool me twice, shame on me."

In our experience, closing the sale is not about gimmickry or trickery. Closing the sale is about helping the customer make a decision to solve a problem or capitalize on an opportunity. We have found the best way to do this is to summarize the benefits your product offers the customer and then ask for the order. In summarizing the benefits, you should match your product's benefits to the customer's most pressing needs. Of course, this assumes you know the customer's most pressing needs. And you do know them because you have asked good questions to identify the needs and you have listened well. So, list each need and then show or describe how the benefits of your product address each need:

Customer Need #1	Your Company's Solution/Benefit
Customer Need #2	Your Company's Solution/Benefit
Customer Need #3	Your Company's Solution/Benefit

Then ask for the order. A soft, non-threatening way to ask for the order is to simply say, "Based on what we have talked about today, do you feel comfortable purchasing our product?"

We All Live by Selling

Robert Lewis Stevenson said, "We all live by selling something." This is especially true for entrepreneurs. Sell, sell, sell, and then close the deal!

Best Practice: Lower the Barriers

Marketing is the art of lowering barriers. Use rock-solid guarantees and free samples to make it comfortable for buyers to buy. Alleviate risk and turn potential buyers into new customers.

A lot more people intend to buy than actually end up buying. Studies show that only about 75% of the people who say they are *certain to buy* an item will follow through and make the purchase. Barriers stand between potential buyers and making purchases, and risk is one of the biggest! Physical, financial, and emotional risk are facts of everyday life. People really don't like to take risks, and as insurance companies already know, people will pay a lot of money to completely eliminate them.

Every time entrepreneurs ask someone to try some new product or service for the first time, they are asking them to take a hefty risk. Entrepreneurs are asking people to do something they instinctively steer clear of. Entrepreneurial products are fighting tremendous odds because they don't have the financial advantages and brand equity of established products with Fortune 500 backing. Entrepreneurs must lower some barriers by first building brand confidence before they can successfully build brand equity.

> # BOOM
> ## THOUGHT 6.1
> *Buying a new product creates anxiety. Buying a new product from a startup creates even more anxiety. Fight to lower purchasing barriers by lowering physical, financial, and emotional risk.*

Matters become worse when entrepreneurs ask customers to pay full price for a new product and live with the consequences, often for years, whether they are satisfied or not. In marketing we talk about buyer's remorse. It is that nagging, empty feeling you get in the pit of your stomach after bringing your big-ticket item home and realizing you are stuck with it, for better or for worse. Fear of making a bad choice is a huge concern for people, and the concern grows hand in hand with the size of the price tag and the lack of warranties and guarantees.

Entrepreneurs often try to overcome buyer reservations by weaving buzzwords like "quality" and "value" into their marketing literature. Lame buzzwords, however, rarely do anything positive for a new product. Steve McKee, president of McKee Wallwork Cleveland, an ad agency specializing in small-budget fast-growth companies, points out that such words have little impact on consumers because of their overuse and ambiguity. He asks us, "What company doesn't say they produce a quality product?" Everyone makes the quality claim; consequently, playing the quality card does not cut through the communications callus. He also reminds us that value "depends on the buyer, on the purchase occasion, and on what features and benefits that value is being judged." Said another way, "best value" is ambiguous and therefore just one more meaningless phrase in an ocean of meaningless marketing hype. It reminds us of an advertisement for one of the big three US automakers featuring a tattooed, rough-and-tumble autoworker telling consumers, "Quality is a hardworking thang." Watching the ad, we weren't convinced the automobiles he was making delivered true quality, and neither were consumers.

People taking risks on buying new products and services are gambling on the fearful unknown. They need revelatory news, credible evidence, and hard facts to move them forward in the buying process. If you want to communicate value, don't just say it: prove it with **trial periods, guarantees,** and **warranties.**

My Product Is Not Nearly as Bad as You Think!

In the early 1980s, Dave Power, chairman of J.D. Power and Associates, started making visits to Hyundai Motors, getting a feel for their attitudes toward customer satisfaction, product quality, and buying behavior. Hyundai executives stated in a matter-of-fact tone that high quality was not an issue, because with a lower price you don't need higher quality. At the time, Hyundai had 70% market share of car sales in Korea.

BOOM
THOUGHT 6.2

Give potential buyers proof and not puffery! Back up product claims with proof they can see, touch, and take to the bank.

It wasn't until Hyundai took on the role of the newcomer, ventured out of Korea, and tried to break into the US automobile market that they learned some hard lessons about quality, consumer risk, and the uphill battle against entrenched competitors. The first Hyundai to sell in the US was the Hyundai Excel. It turns out the Excel was a good name because the car excelled at breakdowns, electrical failures, and rusting body parts. Hyundai vehicles and their owners became the butt of endless jokes about cheapness and poor quality. Back in the day, one of the favorites was, "How do you double the value of a Hyundai? Fill the gas tank."

Hyundai sales in the US were as poor as the quality of their cars. To their credit, Hyundai executives made tremendous efforts to improve every aspect of their cars. They learned the hard way that low price does not compensate for low quality when breaking into a new "red ocean" market.

Fast-forward several years, and the number of problems reported by buyers of new Hyundai automobiles rivaled the low levels reported by buyers of new Hondas and Toyotas. US car buyers, however, were still not getting the message. For startup products, quality does not sell itself. Hyundai executives were frustrated. They knew their quality was much better than what people thought. Hyundai decided a flashy advertising campaign would solve the image problem. A national campaign was launched acknowledging past problems and touting vast quality improvements. The ads seemed to be saying apologetically, "Please, we are not as bad as you think we are!"

Millions were spent, but the quality message still had no traction with the American public. Executives were really getting frustrated and desperate. Then they finally saw the light. Americans needed hard proof, not advertising puffery. Hyundai switched gears and decided to use advertising to spread some good news: a 10-year/100,000-mile warranty compared to the US big three automakers' three-year/36,000-mile warranty. The shocking disparity in warranties got everyone's attention and drove prospective buyers past the risk gap. When buying a Hyundai, consumers now had palpable evidence that they could depend on their new car for at least 10 years. Just as important, Hyundai quality was in fact to the point where it could deliver on the 10-year promise.

In 2006, Hyundai achieved the unthinkable for a lowly, quality-plagued newcomer. It ranked as the #1 non-premium brand on the J.D. Power Quality Survey, edging out both Toyota and Honda. Toyota group vice president and general manager Jim Lentz acknowledged in a news conference, "There's no question that Hyundai is coming on strong and doing a tremendous job . . . they are going to become a bigger and bigger player in the marketplace." Hyundai executives give credit for the quick shift in fortunes to pushing the envelope on warranty. Before the path-breaking 10-year warranty, few noticed the quality improvements or realized that Hyundai had more to offer than just a low price. As the advertising says, "Hyundai . . . rethink everything!"

You'll Love the Free Trial Period, I Guarantee It!

In case anyone missed it earlier, here is a key point worth repeating. Entrepreneurs face an uphill struggle against entrenched competitors and the unrelenting risk-aversion of consumers. Entrepreneurs must do more than look for product sales: entrepreneurs must make product believers.

As a country, we are getting smart about guarantees. It is not a new tactic and the American public has seen just about everything: money-back guarantees, performance guarantees, guarantees for uptime, guarantees for downtime, satisfaction guarantees, guarantees for sunny vacations, even guarantees for handsome, happy, healthy children. We've seen so much, we have developed the power to filter out meaningless guarantees. A good guarantee cuts through into the consumers' consciousness by addressing core uncertainties—that is, it gets right to the heart of the consumers' concerns connected with a product. A good guarantee removes the risk of the unknown, guarantees a key result, and ensures the consumer will be able to achieve a specific and meaningful goal.

BOOM
THOUGHT 6.3
Meaningful product guarantees often address the core concerns of customers and usually cost an entrepreneur only a fraction of sales revenue.

The ubiquitous power strip is a favorite example. What computer around the world is not plugged into a power strip promising protection from power surges and spikes caused by lightning and other electrical nasties? Yet prices for power strips vary widely. Being curious, we asked a power strip manufacturer about the technical differences between the $5 and $150 varieties. She told us there is not much difference inside or out. This was confirmed by Wendell Laidley, president of Zero Surge, Inc. He states, "The assumption that higher-priced surge protectors provide greater effectiveness and reliability is often not valid. Almost all surge protectors priced under $200 rely on the same fundamental MOV components." We read it, but we don't want to believe it!

The difference is in the carefully crafted guarantee. It is not uncommon for the more expensive products to guarantee equipment replacement up to $100,000 or more if the power strip fails to protect it. But, you say, how often can that happen? It turns out it doesn't happen that often at all. According to industry data, the circuits used in most surge protectors will fail once per billion hours of operation due to inadequate protection. That is a lot of hours without failure, offering well over 20,000 customers five years of ironclad protection. Assuming the manufacturer is selling their $3 part for $150, even considering retail margins and other marketing costs, they will earn over $2,500,000 in premiums to buy a new computer for that one customer with a bad surge protector.

APC surge protectors has increased the price of avoiding pain. At a price point of $1500, the list of features for APC's new line of surge-protecting power conditioners is impressive. Aside from a lifetime guarantee against failure and unlimited equipment replacement protection, the APC also has a battery backup to prevent any electrical interruptions to personal computers, network servers, audiovisual gear, or anything else that would suffer possible damage when the power goes out unexpectedly. APC has taken equipment protection guarantees beyond power surge to power loss and increased the price tenfold. Never be afraid to offer creative guarantees or to create products around them. Run the numbers. You will begin to believe, like we do, that guarantees pay back more in building consumer confidence, overcoming competitive barriers, and delivering profits than they cost.

Free Samples Will Solve All the Problems— Or Will They?

Read all of the marketing textbooks about giving a new product a jump-start in the marketplace, and the usual advice is to overcome feelings of consumer risk by offering free samples. Good advice in general, but entrepreneurs operating on small budgets need to be a little more discriminating with their promotional dollars. We recommend entrepreneurs use sampling in only a couple of situations. First, when the new product is naturally addictive. Second, when people are particularly reluctant to try, but are sure to love the product when they do.

The concept of an addictive product is pretty easy to grasp. An unfortunate but memorable example of addictive product sampling comes to us from the tobacco industry. During World War II, tobacco companies like Phillip Morris sent millions of cigarettes to

American soldiers for free. Cigarettes were even included in soldiers' C-rations like food. When the soldiers came home, the tobacco industry had countless loyal customers.

Pinkberry . . . You Can't Eat Just One!

Frozen dessert yogurts, once popular over a decade ago, are making a comeback in a big way. Brands like Pinkberry and Red Mango have found a new formula for making tart frozen yogurt highly addictive. Probiotic yogurts are tart, not very sweet, and fermented in much the same way as beer, wine, and cheese. Pinkberry customers, referring to themselves as groupies, even have a number-one hit tune:

Sorry ice cream, I'm dreaming of a different dessert
Pinkberry shaved ice and frozen yogurt
It doesn't feel like I'm cheating when I'm eating it
Cuz it's healthy, I'm feeling better already

Unlike eating ice cream, these products make people feel good and light. With small servings containing fewer than 90 calories, they really are nutritious and delicious. Customers call it "crack" yogurt, and there is even a YouTube video highlighting its addictiveness, showing family members killing each other just to get more yogurt. These new probiotic yogurts are the kind of products that lend themselves to sampling. When you have an addictive product that can generate a cult-like following with a unique taste and tingly aftertaste sensation, then sample away! Tactics such as two-for-one specials and free trials are very effective when the sampling creates a craving that just one taste won't satisfy.

BOOM
THOUGHT 6.4

Sampling is usually helpful in creating product trial and purchase, but really kicks into high gear when the sample is addictively good.

Free Feels So Right but Can Go So Wrong

Several years ago during the dot-com boom, it was not unusual for an Internet company to be valued according to its site traffic rather than its revenue or profitability. At the time, several companies decided to build their own site traffic by counting, classifying, and summarizing the site traffic of other websites. One such company had tremendous success by offering their real-time traffic reporting for free. They had clients by the thousands and built a business valued at many tens of millions of dollars. But still, they were not making money. They were providing free services.

Ultimately, things changed in the dot-com world and Internet companies needed to start making profits. The traffic-counting company decided it was high time to turn loyal customers into paying customers. They settled on a reasonable price: only $5 per month. But things didn't go as expected. As soon as there was a cost for the service, more than 90% of their customers decided to move on to another supplier. The company was giving away a product that was not uniquely addictive. There were no competitive barriers holding their customers. There were too many similar alternatives readily available and no compelling reason to stay loyal.

Oddly enough, this sort of thing regularly happens. Giving products and services away feels so right—every day is Christmas and you can be Santa Claus—but resist the temptation. A dot-com company called Driveway was launched several years ago as a free service giving away 25 MB of virtual storage space to "clients." At their height there were 9 million registered users, but when free service turned to paid service, few people signed up. There are still free providers out there and paid providers that offer service levels and features that make them unique. Amid the layoffs and cutbacks, Driveway remained a company, but had to reposition itself as a "technology platform provider" and start charging real money.

Free Samples Require Competitive Barriers

Some products have built-in competitive barriers. By nature, they are so uniquely addictive that people will not settle for any substitute. There are not many products on the uniquely addictive list, and we'd guess that most of them are already identified and busy making fortunes for their sellers. Most products need a lot of help to become uniquely addictive.

Good products need the support of high competitive barriers to become great moneymakers. Startups usually have their hands full in making a good product, but putting competitive barriers in place is just as important. It is a sad story, really: so many entrepreneurial companies with great ideas and products being crushed by bigger, better-funded competitors because there were insufficient competitive barriers. Giving away free samples without proper barriers in place makes matters even worse. Without competitive barriers in place, an entrepreneur's free samples build a market that other companies will eventually own and cash in on.

Competitive barriers come in many different varieties. *Picking the right image* to associate with a brand can build enormous competitive barriers. For example, the addictive Marlboro brand has more than nicotine going for it. The brand also has a powerful image synonymous with manliness: the cowboy of the American West. Fact is, Marlboro was first marketed as a women's cigarette under the slogan "Mild as May." Marlboro didn't sell very well as a women's cigarette. The brand really didn't take off until it was reintroduced as a man's cigarette and associated with the cowboy image. At the time, sales were reported to have increased by 5000%.

Vertical integration can lock up the ownership of feed stocks and product parts. Incentives and contracts can allow manufacturers to dominate distribution channels. Technological innovation keeps businesses one or two steps ahead of competitors. These are big barriers to competition, but they almost always cost big bucks that a startup rarely has.

The startup's best bet for building competitive barriers is *creating high switching costs* for customers. Like so many marketing concepts, switching costs are built around perceptions of risk: physical, financial, and emotional. For example, having a business that is the only one that can guarantee there will be no physical risk to the product, the process, or the people involved. Another possibility is selling a product or service that puts a lot of money at risk if the customer were to switch suppliers, such as providing an integrated company-industry informational database. In such a database, mountains of priceless information could be at risk if the data were to be transferred to another supplier or group of suppliers. Emotional risk also can be very powerful. Customers buying a trendy brand may feel the emotional impact of switching to a cheaper, mainstream brand. Of course, this all brings us back to *sharpening the angle*. A great angle builds great competitive barriers!

Clobber Reluctance with a Contest

When purchasing new products or services, people usually have a lot of reasons to be reluctant buyers. But whatever the reason, contests often can help startups triumph over timidity.

Recently a local gym sponsored a contest to win a free personal trainer for a year. Lots of interested but reluctant gym members entered the contest. The gym, however, added a tantalizing twist to the contest. Aside from the one grand prize winner, everyone who entered was a winner. Each member filling out an entry form was offered one free session with a personal trainer. Great idea, because winning puts people in a good mood, the good mood can be amplified by a positive "consumption experience" with the personal trainer, and the positive experience can quickly blossom into a six-month personal training contract.

The gym is not doing a sneaky thing: they are doing a good thing in helping reluctant gym members get firsthand experience with the benefits of personal training. The service will help gym members build confidence and reach their fitness goals faster than if they struggled along on their own, but it is hard to see the value if you are just watching from the sidelines and don't get in the game yourself.

There are many value-added services that startups should allow customers to sample. Customers are understandably reluctant to give a bigger and bigger share-of-wallet to a single supplier. They will need a nudge. Perhaps a contest will be just the incentive they need!

> # BOOM
> ## THOUGHT 6.5
> At trade shows, make sampling a game in which people are rewarded when they can recall a product's key selling points. Make sure everyone walks away with a story as well as a gift.

Sampling Expensive Products

With startup companies, products are sometimes too expensive to give away as free samples. Yet, in many instances sampling still makes sense. Trade shows, home shows, expos, fairs, festivals, and anything else that brings lots of people and like-minded vendors together all provide avenues to offer potential customers hands-on product experience. Trade shows can be some of the most cost-effective marketing entrepreneurs will ever do. Data indicate more than half of the people that attend trade shows purchase one or more products.

In addition to letting people "sample" your expensive products at the trade show, provide some giveaways that reinforce your product distinctions. Make it a game. Reward people with a free gift when they can recite the company slogan or recall your top three selling points. People should walk away from the booth with your story as well as your gift. But beware of people that run from booth to booth collecting no-strings-attached freebies. Create an experience that eliminates freeloaders, but encourages buyers!

Best Practice: Price for Profit

Pricing seems like the easiest part of marketing, but don't be fooled. Pricing is hard to get right and pricing incentives are often misapplied. Look for the right opportunities to use short-term, limited-time pricing incentives to motivate purchases. Run value well ahead of price.

Several years ago we had the opportunity to sit down and talk with a retired manager of a Coca-Cola bottling plant. Coca-Cola is one of those marketing juggernauts every entrepreneur should be interested in. Worldwide annual per capita consumption of Coca-Cola products has grown from 30 servings in the mid-1980s to 50 servings in the mid-1990s to currently more than 75 servings. We wanted to know how Coca-Cola did it. What is it about

Are You Selling Coke or Toilet Paper? Pricing Tactics Depend on the Answer!

Having more Coca-Cola on hand accelerates its consumption. The same cannot be said for toilet paper. Coca-Cola uses motivational pricing to get more of their products in the home and permanently increase consumption rates.

© 2009, JupiterImages

the product and its marketing that creates such phenomenal success? How is it that every man, woman, and child in North America drinks on average over 400 servings of Coca-Cola products each year? That adds up to more than 25 gallons for every person in North America!

To answer our questions, the retired manager started off the conversation in an unexpected direction. "The thing is," he said, "selling Coca-Cola is not like selling toilet paper." We appreciated the differences between the two products, but didn't grasp the significance. So we asked for some clarification. We found out that Coca-Cola is one of those magical products that the more of it people have on hand, the faster they will consume it. That is, the more of it people have in their homes, the more occasions they find to drink it. People drink it for breakfast, drink it while they drive into work, drink it as a pick-me-up when at work, drink it with lunch, drink it as a reward when returning home from work, drink it with dinner, even drink it to settle themselves before going to bed. Coca-Cola has a magic that toilet paper simply doesn't. The consumption rate and usage occasions for toilet paper do not change, or at least stay very stable, no matter how much of it a person has on hand. In fact, with products like toilet paper, consumers often concentrate on ways to use less of it and not how to use more of it.

Coca-Cola executives understand the magic of their product and use motivational pricing to leverage the magic to its full advantage. At what appear to be almost randomly selected dates, consumers can purchase Coca-Cola products on price promotion with offers such as two-for-one, temporary price reduction, and more rarely price-off coupons. Once in the home, family members can't resist it and demand more and more of it even when it is not being sold on promotion.

If your product is like Coca-Cola, then pricing promotions not only build sales in the short term, but will increase overall consumpation rates. You will be giving away a little profit now to earn greater and greater returns in the future. If, however, your product is like toilet paper, then pricing promotions simply give away profits now and in the future as people "stock up" at the bargain price. You may be winning the battle for market share, but are surely losing the battle for profitability. A quick inspection of a few storage shelves in our homes proves that we understand the concept: they are fully stocked with paper products sold on promotion.

Not Selling Coca-Cola? Then Learn More About Pricing!

Coca-Cola sets their price to be competitive with other premium-branded carbonated soda drinks, offers a variety of temporary price promotions, and then they're done. Your pricing decision may not be so easy.

Arriving at an appropriate pricing policy requires that we understand three things particularly well: our costs, our competitors, and our customers. Most companies are pretty good at figuring out their costs and use an accounting approach to pricing. Accountants calculate the cost and then add on the margin needed to make the return demanded by management or investors. Eureka, they've found their price!

The trouble with cost-plus, accounting-based pricing is that product costs are irrelevant to buyers. People don't care about how much it costs to manufacture and distribute a product. That is our problem and constant preoccupation and not theirs! It is very easy to price a product too high using cost-plus pricing. For startup products, the cost-plus price may be significantly higher than the reference prices that people see day-in-day-out in the marketplace. In which case, our brilliant product idea better be incredibly brilliant or it won't sell at all. But then again, your product is unique.

Four Pricing Approaches	Golden Goose	Value
Cost-plus, i.e., calculating cost then adding a "fair" margin, is the most commonly used pricing approach. Hire a good accountant and this pricing approach becomes very easy. However, because product costs are irrelevant to buyers, cost-plus pricing often will set a price too high or too low, resulting in lower than expected sales or reduced profits.	Know own costs, and a lot about customer value.	Know own costs, and a lot about customer value and prices/costs of competitors.
	Cost-Plus	**Competitive**
	Know own costs, but not much about competitors or customers.	Know own costs, and a lot about prices of competitors.

We hear the claim all the time, but the truth is people base similarity by making comparisons of function and not form. So before making the claim of uniqueness, please start by looking around for functional competitors, and then benchmark their prices.

Reference Prices and Competitive Pricing

Competitive pricing is a much better approach than cost-plus pricing because it takes into account what competitors are charging and what people are paying in specific buying situations. The first step in applying the competitive pricing approach is tackling the question of reference prices. To illustrate how reference prices work when making purchasing decisions, Richard Thaler[6] administered two versions of a questionnaire to a large group of consumers. One version uses the phrases shown below in parentheses. The other version uses the phrases shown below in brackets.

"You are lying on the beach on a hot day. All you have to drink is ice water. For the last hour you have been thinking about how much you would enjoy a nice cold bottle of your favorite brand of beer. A companion gets up to go make a phone call and offers to bring back a beer from the only nearby place where beer is sold (a fancy resort hotel) [a small, run-down grocery store]. He says that he will buy the beer if it costs as much or less than the price you state. But if it costs more than the price you state he will not buy it. You trust your friend, and there is no possibility of bargaining with the (bartender) [store owner]. What price do you tell him?"

In 1984 dollars, the median response for the resort was $2.50, whereas the median response for the small grocery store was $1.50. Thaler points out that people are willing to pay more at the resort because the reference price in that context is higher. People are just used to seeing higher prices at fancy resort hotels than they are at small mom-and-pop grocery stores. A $2.50 beer at the resort is acceptable. A $2.50 beer at a small grocery store is gouging.

When we look for reference prices, we want to identify similar functionality of products as well as a similar buying context. Once we identify the relevant reference prices, we can set our own price at a discount or a premium, depending on the extra risk and/or extra value that potential buyers see in our product. As a reminder,

---

[6]"Mental Accounting and Consumer Choice," by Richard Thaler, in *Marketing Science* (1985), Vol. 4, pp. 199–214

there are three types of buying risks that people consider: financial (will this purchase end up in a financial loss), physical (will this purchase end up physically harming me or my family), and psychological (will this purchase make me look bad to my community and peer group). High risk sets a low floor on price. There are also three types of value that people consider: functional (will this purchase give me more features and functionality than I now have), economic (will this purchase save me money compared to what I have now), and emotional (will this product make me feel more accepted, admired, assured, accomplished, and/or delighted with life than I am now). High value sets a high ceiling on price.

Don't Kill the Golden Goose

In Aesop's fable, a poor farmer and his wife discover a goose that can lay golden eggs. They sell the golden eggs and become prosperous, but also become impatient and greedy. Not content with slowly harvesting the eggs, the couple kills and cuts open the goose to get all of the gold inside. Of course, there is no gold to be found and the couple soon sinks back into poverty.

The more businesses understand about creating functional, economic, and particularly emotional value, the higher potential there is for making profits. However, the potential for this type of financial success doesn't come without danger. Every business that finds a "golden goose" is in danger of charging too high a price which in turn attracts competitors willing to deliver similar products for less money. Businesses using golden goose pricing understand how to create customer value, but underestimate the ability and resourcefulness of competitors.

Successful entrepreneurs have a sense of how to run value well ahead of price. Dave Wilson started selling audio loudspeakers more than 20 years ago. From the beginning, his speakers and marketing approach had a knack for creating tremendous customer value. Today his range of products sells for between $25,000 and $125,000. That is right. A pair of speakers weighing in at over 2,000 pounds, called the Alexandria X-2 in case you are in the market, sells for $125,000. In a

BOOM
THOUGHT 6.6

If you find a golden goose, be patient and harvest your gold slowly. Capturing every cent of value will attract big competitors that will undermine your prices and your success.

product review, one audiophile remarks, "That's a ridiculous amount of money, but somehow, as I was helping set up these speakers in my living room, I was not at all bothered by the price." Wilson Audio has a long waiting list of people wanting to buy his speakers, even though many comparably priced products as well as less costly alternatives are readily available. He knows how to create value and run value well ahead of price. He has the patience to slowly harvest those golden eggs!

Dave recently met with a group of business consultants and entrepreneurs who harangued him about his pricing policy. They reasoned, "There is a long waiting list; therefore the price must be too low. There is more money to be made." What the panel of experts did not realize, however, is that a long waiting list is a big part of the value in the strange world of audiophile one-upsmanship. Dave Wilson was polite and respectful, but declined to raise his prices. Sidestepping greed is a key success factor.

Value Pricing to the Rescue

Value pricing doesn't necessarily mean charging a low price. It means charging a price that is high enough to capture a lot of customer value, but not so high as to encourage competition. DuPont's pricing approach for titanium dioxide is a classic example of value pricing.

Titanium dioxide is all around us. It is the most-used white pigment in the world. It is added to paint, plastic, paper, food, toothpaste, cosmetics, and numerous skin care products. There are two ways to manufacture titanium dioxide pigment. With the first method, called the sulfate process, titanium dioxide is bathed in sulfuric acid. With the second method, called the chloride process, titanium dioxide is bathed in chlorine. The sulfate process fixed costs (factory) are low, but the marginal costs (production) are high. The chloride process fixed costs (factory) are high, but the marginal costs (production) are low. To make the story just a bit more complex, the pigment grade yielded by the chloride process is much better than that from the sulfate process.

DuPont uses the chloride process, and when entering the market as the world's largest titanium dioxide manufacturer, had a tough pricing decision. Should they set the price low because their production costs were the lowest in the industry? Should they set

Full Value	
Value Price	
Marginal Cost	

Where Is the Value Price?

The *value price* runs value well ahead of price and does not attract an onslaught of big competitors.

the price high because their pigment grade was the best in the industry? If they chose a high price, how high should they go? Ultimately, DuPont decided more profit was better than less profit and consequently set a high price, but they were careful not to set it so high as to encourage competitors using the sulfate process to build new chloride-process factories. DuPont did their homework to uncover competitive cost structures and financial resources before deciding on a price. They wanted to make sure DuPont profitability wasn't so large as to attract direct competition. Pricing high enough to capture significant customer value without "killing the golden goose" takes thorough research into every facet of the marketplace equation: own costs, customer value, competitor prices, and competitor costs.

The Lowdown on Lowering Prices

A company selling custom-built cars asked for help in designing a motivational pricing plan. Their cars sell for as little as $40,000 to well over $125,000 depending on the model, parts, and options. The owner, however, was convinced an untapped "low-end" market existed for the cars starting at a $25,000 price point. Should they just start selling $25,000 cars, if they could still make money? Should the cars be the same as their current offerings? If different, how should they be changed?

This sort of thinking should sound familiar albeit perverse. The golden goose is being threatened by the axe yet again. This time, rather than setting a dangerously high price, it is dropping prices to pursue a dream of volume-profits from tapping into a price-sensitive "mass market" that may kill the golden goose. Like it or not, price indicates quality. People buying exotic sports cars understandably want the cars to hold value so that they retain their exclusivity or perhaps so down the road they can sell the car for a premium and try out a new toy. So as not to upset the apple cart, a price drop must be accompanied by a good set of reasons. We recommended a sweat-equity version of the car with obvious markings or nameplate identifying it as a second-tier product.

What is true for exotic sports cars is true for pizza. Perhaps you recall our example of the Pizza Hut BIGFOOT Pizza—the two square feet of pizza cut into 21 pieces sold at a bargain price. The product was designed to tap into the large and growing low-end pizza market dominated by Little Caesars. But there were problems. Little Caesars pizza is cheap by design, whereas Pizza Hut pizza is the premium alternative to the quick gut-fill. Millions were spent developing and marketing BIGFOOT, and millions of dollars were lost as Pizza Hut customers switched from buying the premium Pizza Hut pizza to the BIGFOOT or stopped buying Pizza Hut pizza altogether, disappointed and angered by the perceived decline in Pizza Hut product quality. Sadly, BIGFOOT led to hard-to-swallow big losses and taught them a tough lesson. Cutting price to buy your way into a market may not work. It is a lesson every entrepreneur needs to consider. Simply making and selling a product more cheaply does not guarantee success!

What are the lessons learned about motivational pricing? First, pricing decisions, just like decisions about every other element of the marketing mix, need to be decisions for the long term, because they will have long-term consequences. If you sell a product like Coca-Cola, use temporary price promotions to get more product into more homes to permanently drive up annual per capita consumption rates. If you sell other types of products, pricing incentives need to be selected in a way that doesn't undermine customer value, increase price sensitivity, or allow people to stock up. Second, once a price is established in the marketplace, it takes a lot of justification to move it up or down. Move it up too fast and people will cry foul. Move it down without some good explanation and people will sense a loss in quality or even resent what they may perceive as higher-than-necessary prices they've paid in the past.

Best Practice: Choose the Right Moment

Deliver the right product when and where people want it the most. Earning a premium depends on timing and context. Your choice of marketing channel often determines the price people will pay and whether the product will sell.

The Fan Cost Index (FCI) tracks how much it costs a family of four to attend a major league sporting event around the country, whether it is baseball, football, basketball, or hockey. For many years, the number-one team in the country has been the New England Patriots. Its FCI hovers just below $600. The LA Lakers aren't far behind at over $450. Even a Red Sox game will set back a family of four well over $300.

A cost of $150 a head to see a Patriots football game in person that can be watched from the comfort of one's home for next to nothing begs the question, "Just what is going on here?" Let's break down the costs: $120 for a ticket, $40 for parking, $5 for a program, $15 for a cap, $3.50 for a hot dog, $4.00 for a soda, and $7.50 for a beer. The hot dog, soda, and beer are pricey, yet fans stand in long lines to buy. How can entrepreneurs tap into that type of marketing mojo?

Once an entrepreneur has a great product, there are lots of marketing success factors to consider, but we have come to appreciate that none have greater influence over price, closing sales, and long-term success than picking the right marketing channel. The topic of marketing channels can be complicated and remarkably boring, with considerations about power in the channel, whether one should use exclusive, selective, or intensive distribution, and many other nuances about mixing, adding, or pruning channel types or members. Nevertheless, we need to spend some time thinking about channels because they are so important.

The fine points of managing marketing channels are fascinating subjects for Fortune 500 marketers, but out of necessity entrepreneurs must focus their attention only on a single point: marketing channels are just devices to get a product sold and at a price that guarantees a reasonable profit. At the risk of setting back the marketing literature 20 years, we will repeat what one executive of a billion-dollar corporation had to say about the topic: "The better we get at partnering with people in our marketing channel, the faster we train our new competitors." A startup cannot afford to train new competitors. Entrepreneurs already have enough competitive hurdles. Don't think of a channel member—for example, a distributor—as a partner. To put it bluntly, they are just a tool and we must pick the right tool for the job.

Picking the Right Distribution Tool

We have three simple criteria for picking the right distribution tool. Put the product where people are (1) ready to buy, (2) able to pay, and (3) know that good alternatives are out of reach. Let's take Red Bull energy drink as an example. A manager at an Atlanta bar believes it is no mystery why energy drinks like Red Bull are bestsellers. She says, "If I'm tired I just grab a can and I'm good to go . . . it just makes me feel alert, awake." Spokeswoman for Red Bull, Kim Peterson, says the beverage is uniquely uplifting because it contains vitamins and amino acids such as taurine, evoking images of Taurus the bull. Nutritionists say that it is uniquely uplifting because it contains a high concentration of sugar and caffeine.

> # BOOM
> ## THOUGHT 6.7
>
> *Increase earnings by taking your product benefit to where people need it and are able to pay for it and where all good alternatives are out of reach.*

Red Bull demographics show that drinkers are predominantly single males between the ages of 15 and 24, with use dropping off sharply for anyone over 34 years old. Red Bull is the drink of choice for the active guy. At our age, we have to wonder why young men would ever need an energy boost, but whatever the reason, clinical tests do show that it improves athletic performance and can keep people alert when operating on too little sleep. Consequently, Red Bull Vending recommends placing their machines in gyms, office buildings, strip malls, schools, and universities. Service stations are encouraged to keep big chests of iced-down Red Bull near their cash registers, particularly during holiday weekends, to refresh tired drivers. Red Bull also appears at "extreme sports" venues. Evidently modern-day youth need to have an extra boost of energy just to watch high-energy sports, or perhaps they want to get as ramped-up as the athletes they admire.

Energy is at the core of the Red Bull value proposition. When thinking about marketing channels, executives look to distributing Red Bull energy where the profits are. Agree or not with the product, we have to hand it to Red Bull for getting their brand of energy to where active guys need it, are able to pay, and find that good alternatives are out of reach.

Play to Strength with the Marketing Channel

When introducing the concept of the *sweet spot,* we described Del Sol, a terrific entrepreneurial company that sells hats, T-shirts, shorts, sunglasses, body glitter, and even nail polish that change from subdued to bright color when exposed to bright sun. Starting from a small cart in a Salt Lake City shopping mall, the entrepreneurs soon discovered that where they distributed and sold the product made a big difference in sales and customer satisfaction. USA locations are concentrated up and down the Eastern Seaboard and in Hawaii and California. There is not much franchise activity in the nose-to-the-grindstone Midwest or rain-soaked Northwest. Worldwide locations are concentrated in sunny resort towns. Del Sol distributes where people wear and want to show off hats, T-shirts, shorts, sunglasses, body glitter, and nail polish. Places sunny enough to fully energize the color-change technology. Places where product strengths can really shine.

In contrast to Del Sol, consider a startup that literally was selling a better mousetrap made out of plastic tubing. The trap was clean, chemical-free, and safe and killed by suffocating the mouse. The only trouble was, users reported the high-priced trap hopped around like a "Mexican jumping bean" with the suffocating mouse struggling to get out. If users couldn't stand to hear the mouse struggling, they had to pick up the trap with the live mouse inside and find some way to release it without getting "creeped out." Makers of the better mousetrap decided it would be a perfect fit for women because it was safe, clean, and chemical-free. After a lot of work, they landed distribution deals with a national chain of home improvement centers and mass marketing outlets. As one might expect, the mousetrap was priced too high relative to other readily available mousetraps in the home improvement centers to be purchased frequently or repurchased—due to the emotionally disturbing clanging and banging of the suffocating mouse.

To make matters worse, a huge delivery of new mousetraps missed the strict delivery schedule of a mass marketing outlet. The traps were refused and needless to say, the product failed. The target and channel selection highlighted weakness and did not play to strength. Even a "better mousetrap" cannot succeed unless it is placed in front of customers that are ready to buy, are able to pay, and do not have good alternatives readily available.

Avoid Marketing Channels That Rub a Sore Spot

When picking marketing channels, go with alternatives that highlight what your product and company do best. Avoid marketing channels that rub a sore spot. That is, avoid channels that uncover or accentuate product or company vulnerabilities.

Signing on a big distributor is the dream of every startup, but as the "better mousetrap" experience described above points out, the dream can quickly turn into a nightmare if the channel really doesn't "play to strength." Big distributors make big demands of their vendors.

Startups try to meet the big demands of big distributors, but often get swallowed up in the process. As an example, recall the clever little product Chap-Grip, "lip balm on a leash." It lets users clip their lip balm to their keys, ski jacket, backpack, etc. The Chap-Grip startup team worked day and night, mortgaged homes, and called in all of their family and friends to meet a tough delivery schedule with a huge order for a mass merchandiser. The entrepreneurs delivered on time, and they expected the retailer to deliver the payment on time. It didn't happen, and as the overdue days mounted up, so did the frustration and financial damage. Ultimately the mass merchandiser didn't like the tone of the demands for payment being made by Chap-Grip, and so they returned all the merchandise. The choice of channel uncovered financial weakness and led to a disaster from which the startup has never fully recovered. Big distributors often pay their vendors slowly, which can put a real strain on chronically undercapitalized entrepreneurs.

Another cautionary tale comes from the sad case of a small entrepreneurial company manufacturing water-weenies. The water-weenie is an American institution. It is a long inflatable tube for children to ride as a power boat drags them around a lake or reservoir. What could be more fun than a water-weenie? On the other hand, one can only imagine that the water-weenie itself must take a pretty hard beating from the water and its young riders. And when things get packed up for the return home, the water-weenie probably doesn't get the best of care.

The water-weenie entrepreneurs decided to sell the product through a national chain of "club stores." They sold thousands of dollars of inventory, but toward the end of the summer season, something strange started happening. A huge number of the water-weenies started coming back. Some had small leaks or tears, but most were perfectly fine. It seems that many buyers had taken advantage of the retailer's liberal return policies and decided to take back the water-weenie for a refund rather than try to store it until next summer. Shoot, they could pick up a new one next year. The startup was left holding the bag for thousands of dollars of returned merchandise.

Startups have at least three sore spots to consider when picking a marketing channel. (1) Startups run on a shoestring budget. Don't bet the farm on a distributor that is unlikely to pay promptly. (2) Startups rarely have the capability to meet tight schedules with huge deliveries. Manufacturing capacity is bound to be small, and few entrepreneurs own their own trucking rigs or keep professional drivers on the payroll. Increase sales patiently, or at least work with marketing channels that understand and are willing to work around an entrepreneur's limitations. (3) Startups can't afford "no questions asked" return policies. Sure, if a product is broken or doesn't perform as advertised, then it should be repaired or replaced. On the other hand, no entrepreneur wants to deal with a water-weenie disaster.

Online Marketing: the Perfect Channel?

In many ways, e-commerce can be an entrepreneur's best choice for a marketing channel. E-tailing is the antithesis of big retailing. Payment comes when the product is purchased, not when the retailer decides to pay. There is no need to deliver huge quantities of product on a tight delivery schedule. The startup only needs enough product to meet current demand. In addition, the startup can set its own return policy, control its pricing, and be more creative than the big retailer with sales promotion and merchandising.

All of these e-tailer advantages, however, come at a cost. With e-commerce, good alternatives are only a click away. Forget about success, if you are selling a product that can easily be found on other websites at a lower price. Online marketing requires a unique

BOOM
THOUGHT 6.8

E-tailing is tough. With tens of thousands of e-commerce sites, online buyers must immediately see what is being sold, get excited about distinctive benefits, and have a reason to buy now.

product backed up with an engaging sales pitch. The big three problems of e-commerce sites are (1) no traffic, (2) lots of traffic but few interested buyers, and (3) abandoned shopping carts, which can run as high as 80% on some sites.

Internet buyers come with a purpose. If they don't see a reason to be at a site or stay on a site, they will pass you by in a matter of seconds. Internet buyers are restless. If the information they want is hidden, they won't hunt for it. Internet buyers are skeptical. Forget pushy tactics and hyperbole. Let the facts speak for themselves. It is up to you to provide real proof and a clear reason to buy now.

Get Out of the Way of the Purchase

If a startup selects an online marketing channel, it must get out of the way of the purchase. For example, the site visitor must immediately see what is being sold, have answers to their questions about the product at their fingertips so that they can get excited about its distinctive benefits, and have a reason to buy now via limited time offers promising free or upgraded shipping, temporary price reductions, free accessories, etc. Make the site easy to navigate by eliminating page scrolling, reducing the number of clicks to get key information, having a one-click buying option, and minimizing distractions like unneeded pictures, disorganized text, or too many icons. Be upfront with the costs, shipping policies, return policies, and guarantees. Surprises at the shopping cart or after the sale not only hurt your chances to make a sale, but may create a lot of ill will that can quickly spread throughout the online community.

Best Practice: Augment Your Core

Tap into unseen revenue streams by finding new products to complement your original product. Earn more dollars by augmenting and amplifying through launching exciting line and brand extensions that can take a startup business to new heights.

Are You Selling the Whole Product?

Every product has three components. Each plays a role in generating new sales and return business.

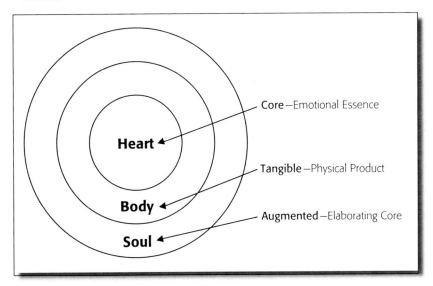

Philip Kotler, the famous marketing professor and practitioner from the Kellogg School, separates every product into three components: core, tangible, and augmented. Taking some liberty with his framework, we describe the core product as its emotional essence and the tangible product as the physical expression of the core. Thinking about McDonald's restaurants, the core product is Family, Fun, and Friends. The tangible product is the Big Mac Meal, i.e., two all-beef patties, cheese, special sauce, lettuce, pickle, onion on sesame seed bun with fries and a medium drink. Perhaps in this example you sense, as we do, that a tangible product has no heart or strategic direction unless it also has a core. Similarly, a tangible product can be pretty boring and has very little room for growth without augmentation and amplification.

At McDonald's, there has always been a whole lot of augmentation and amplification going on. Next time you visit a McDonald's restaurant, you might want to look around and think for a moment of all the ways marketers have elaborated on the theme of Family, Fun, and Friends. The signs of augmentation and amplification are everywhere: cheerful Golden Arches, colorful Happy

Meals, Ronald McDonald and all his friends, quick and friendly service, upbeat advertising. The list goes on and on.

However, even McDonald's makes a mistake now and then. Do you remember the Arch Deluxe? It was launched in 1996 in what is reported to be one of the most expensive advertising campaigns of the 90s. Analysts have estimated that the research, production, and marketing for the Arch Deluxe ran upwards of $300 million. Touted as "the burger with the grown-up taste," it was a commercial failure and selected as one of the worst new products of the year.

As sandwiches go, it probably was a pretty good burger, but advertising showed children turning up their noses and making sour faces at the Arch Deluxe. It didn't take long for the consuming public to get the message. The family fun was gone. Sales dropped. McDonald's shifted advertising messages away from the sneering children, but it was too late to save the line extension. The Arch Deluxe was positioned in direct conflict with the heart of the franchise. Managers desperately wanted to expand sales into adult-oriented food, but allowed an ad agency to throw a wrench into the McDonald's magical formula for success.

Augmentation via line extension adds new products in the same category to compliment the existing line of products. They work best when they directly support the core or emotional essence of the business. Consequently, the success or failure of a line extension is up to you, the marketer. McDonald's now successfully sells a variety of adult-oriented salads. Having learned their Arch Deluxe lesson, McDonald's positions these salads as adding to the fun rather than spoiling the fun for its younger customers.

Line Extension vs. Brand Extension

Marketers make distinctions between line extensions and brand extensions. Both can be powerful ways to open up new revenue streams. Honda clearly demonstrates the difference between line and brand extensions. It was a line extension when Honda launched the Accord in 1976 as a follow-up to the Civic, which was launched in 1973. On the other hand, when Honda launched products outside of the "moving vehicle" product category, such as power generators, lawnmowers, and snowblowers, Honda executives were launching brand extensions. When augmenting via line and brand extensions, we must stay true to the heart of our business. For

Honda Motors, all of the augmentation has stayed true to reliability, practicality, and value.

Dangers of Extension

The two dangers of line and brand extensions are confusion and dilution. There is a story about an immigrant from an Eastern European country who stood crying in front of the ready-to-eat cereal aisle in an American supermarket. An observer who knew the immigrant thought his tears must be tears of joy because of the blessings of now living in such a wonderful, bounteous country. But when asked why he was crying, he said that he was completely confused and frustrated by the number of products. In his mother country there was only cereal, not 100 different kinds of cereal to choose from.

Product line proliferation causes confusion. And while it doesn't cause many of us to break down in tears, it does cause consumer frustration and indecision. Taken to the extreme—and large companies have taken us there—the added costs of maintaining a shelf full of line extensions often are not justified by the incremental revenues.

Dilution is the kissing cousin of confusion. Brand extensions leverage brand equity, and brand equity is like a bathtub full of brand magic. The bathtub can be filled by advertising and positive consumption experiences, and can be drained by spreading the magic too thin by launching a wide assortment of products competing in an equally wide assortment of product categories. When it comes to line and brand extensions, no one has generally determined how much is too much. However, we can give you an example of one business taking the concept too far.

Priceline.com developed a business model based on people who name their own prices for assets like airline seats, hotel rooms, and rental cars that just sit idle earning no revenue unless someone is using them. Name-your-own-price was a stroke of genius that benefited the buyer—cheap travel—as well as the seller, who could earn some revenue from idle assets.

Priceline put together a great package of cheap travel combined with cheesy promotions featuring Star Trek's Captain Kirk, William Shatner. If it wasn't a combination made in heaven, it was a combination made at least in outer space. Business was going well, and Priceline decided the brand known for cheap travel could also dominate cheap groceries and cheap gasoline. Didn't Priceline own cheap? But this was extending Priceline too far. Grocery shoppers could find bargains, but had to spend all day driving around from store to store to fill their grocery carts. Gasoline shoppers also ran over some inconvenient speed bumps. Customers paid for gasoline online, waited for Priceline gas cards to arrive in the mail, and then had to find a gas station that would honor them. The hassles and ill will created by these misguided new product ideas quickly drained a lot of the Priceline magic out of its brand equity bathtub!

Creating Consumer Interest with Augmentation

We are always interested in following promotional campaigns for local car dealerships. Do they know how to create excitement by using a clever augmentation? We'll let you be the judge. One group of local car dealerships is operated by the owner of a sports franchise. Frequently, when customers buy a new car from him, they will receive a ticket package to watch several games in the nosebleed seats, i.e., those hard-to-sell seats that Cub Scout troops usually buy in bulk. Another dealership gives away a free ski rack with the purchase of every new four-wheel-drive SUV sold leading up to the winter ski season. Yet another dealership gives away an internally mounted TV/DVD combination with several Disney movies with the sale of every "family-style" minivan.

BOOM
──THOUGHT 6.9──

Riding the wave of interest by augmenting the core of a successful product through selling a complementary product or service can be the fastest way to find entrepreneurial success.

One of these promotions is not like the other. The first promotion may work for sports fanatics who don't have the budget to buy their own game tickets and enjoy sitting in the upper deck with the Cub Scouts. The other two promotions augment the core. The free ski rack amplifies the excitement and adventure of winter skiing facilitated by the purchase of a large four-wheel-drive vehicle. The free TV/DVD and Disney movies amplify the fun and togetherness of taking road trips with the kids in the family minivan.

We've seen dealerships try about everything with promotional giveaways. They have offered sundry items such as a dozen golf balls, movie tickets, a popular movie DVD, a big bag of candy, an autographed picture of a celebrity, etc., for taking a test drive. In addition to cheap financing, the current rage is to offer free gasoline with the purchase of a new vehicle. Research shows that such efforts raise the long-term price sensitivity of consumers. Not a good thing. To get the full value out of a promotion and a premium price for your product, augment your core.

Another way to think about successful augmentation is to add products that *heighten the delight* surrounding the original product. For example, let's say that you sell carnivorous plants. A great way to *heighten the delight* is by selling "pet supplies" for the plant, such as miniature bones and gravestones to put in the pot with the plant, freeze-dried flies to feed the plant, a "food corral" to collect bugs, or even a spray bottle to "bathe" your plant after a big dinner. In many cases, the complementary products earn more profits than the original product!

Review Questions

Define with Five

Define the following vocabulary words using five words or less.

1. Benefit

   _____

2. Rejection

   _____

3. Golden Goose Price

   _____

4. Augmentation

   _____

5. Line Extension

   _____

Question the Answer

Answer each phrase below in the form of a question.

1. If there is one single secret to super successful entrepreneurs, this is it.

   _____

2. Matching the benefits of your product offering to the needs and wants of your customers.

   _____

3. Ready to buy, able to pay, and alternatives out of reach.

_____

4. Feelings such as being admired, accepted, and assured that tend to set a high ceiling on price.

_____

5. Often determines the price people will pay and whether the product will sell.

_____

Smarter than an Entrepreneur

Name the product or venture that reinforces or violates a Boom Start best practice.

1. By using value-added resellers, this startup gained instant market access and credibility.

_____

2. Quickly built their business with samples of addictive "crack" yogurt.

_____

3. A virtual-storage company that learned what millions want for free, only a few will purchase with cold hard cash.

_____

4. A long waiting list is an important value creator for this company's $125k audio speakers.

_____

5. Have carefully selected marketing channels to energize sales and command high prices.

_____

come back to

SuperLaws in Action

Augmenting a product by selling complementary products and services can be a key to becoming profitable and reaping the benefits of your great ideas.

Activity: Suggest how you can "ride the wave" of success by augmenting the following list of popular products with complementary products and/or services.

POPULAR PRODUCT	COMPLEMENTARY PRODUCT	COMPLEMENTARY SERVICE
Adobe Photoshop		
Legos		
Bratz Dolls		
Altoids		
Matchbox Cars		

Startup Audit

We believe entrepreneurs can improve their new business, and increase their chance of success, by aligning and shaping it using the SuperLaws and Best Practices as their guide. Take a look at how companies have used the Startup Audit to accelerate their success and then try out some audit ideas for your own new business!

We are sorry to say that most new products violate the SuperLaws of entrepreneurial success and often fail. Starting with a Booz, Allen, Hamilton study[1] in the 1980s, research shows again and again that new products have about a one in 10 chance of success. We are not alarmed by the low percent of success. The statistic only means one thing. Finding a successful angle is a numbers game combined with learning and applying the right laws and tactics. The more times we try, the more we learn, and the better chances we have for success. Out of the estimated 20,000 new product launches each year, more than 2,000 will go on to be commercial successes. There is a lot of failure in the marketplace, but there also is a lot of success!

Entrepreneurs cannot afford to spend years perfecting a product idea. To identify a winner, they need to get the ideas out quickly and involve early-adopting customers in the design process. We admit the thought of putting out a less-than-perfect product is painful, but the prospect of never striking gold, when gold is all around us, should be even more painful for success-driven entrepreneurs.

---

[1] *New Products Management for the 1980s* by Booz, Allen, and Hamilton (1982)

Measure the WOW! Factor

A number of years ago, Ken Hakuta, aka Dr. Fad, was asked how he knew that the *wacky wallwalker* toy was going to be a hit. He responded with the surprising comment, "It's really pretty easy, I show people the new product and look to see if they tilt their head slightly to the left and say WOW. If they do, I've got another hit!" At first glance, the "wow measure" seems too simplistic to be a reliable indicator of future success. With R&D firms spending millions of dollars each year testing their new products, how can the evaluation process be reduced to a single word—WOW?

After spending over 10 years investigating and developing successful competitive angles ourselves, we think Dr. Fad is absolutely right. Products and services with the WOW! Factor have something unique and remarkable with stopping power to shock, surprise, delight, and in particular, arouse curiosity. Measuring the WOW! Factor doesn't take a sophisticated questionnaire or Ph.D. in psychology.

When you meet people you feel are in the target audience for the product, start by asking the WOW! Question, i.e., "On a scale of 1 to 10, where 1 means the product isn't very good (stinks) and 10 means the product is great (makes you pull out your credit card), how good is this new product?" If the average rating is above 7.5, congratulations, you have a winner. Go for it; you've got the WOW! Factor and a potential hit if the market opportunity is large enough. If the WOW! Factor is between 5 and 7.5, there is still hope; sharpen the angle. If the WOW! Factor is 5 or below, then people are just being nice to you and don't want to hurt your feelings. There is no WOW! Factor. You really need to go back to the drawing board and redouble your R&D—ripoff and design—efforts!

Along with measuring the WOW! Factor, test to see if you've found a *Love Group* by asking people you believe are in the target audience additional questions such as, "Who would be interested in this type of product?" and "How would they use it?" Then listen and watch. Do you hear some excitement in their voices or see it in their faces? If you're not hearing or seeing anything out of the ordinary, then either the idea, your description of the idea, or the target audience is off the mark. Continue to work on the description and refining the audience, but don't invest a lot of time, energy, or money in building the product until you hit the WOW! Factor and find a WOW! Audience.

I See WOW! Factor

Sub Zero Ice Cream is an example of a product with the WOW! Factor. Jerry Hancock is turning his degree in chemistry into a fun experience for families wanting to create an ice cream experiment. Customers can add fruit, cookies, caramel, or butterscotch to mixtures of either vanilla or chocolate, then watch as liquid nitrogen flows over the ingredients in a large stainless steel tank. Fog rises from the tank as the mixture freezes, and presto, like magic, you have your own freshly made, personalized serving of ice cream in only 60 seconds!

BOOM
THOUGHT 7.1

Once you've found a product with the WOW! Factor, get it to market quickly. Early customers excited by the product concept can be very forgiving and generous.

As one might imagine, the product and process still have some imperfections. What is the right amount of liquid nitrogen? What sorts of mix-ins work best? How can less skilled and conscientious workers be trained to perform the magic safely? But while these questions get answered, Jerry is already out there following his dream, and amazed customers are helping with their dollars and their comments.

Help Imperfections Go Down Easy

Having a strong WOW! Factor goes a long way in creating a forgiving attitude among customers, but we can do more. Cal State Professor Matthew Lancellotti suggests four things entrepreneurs can do to prepare and cushion customers for the product imperfections that inevitably crop up.

1. **Admit to imperfection**
   Communicate that you make continuing improvements to the product, purchasing process, and service system. You expect to find ways to improve.

2. **Help customers help themselves**

   Use reading materials, web-based tutorials, or online forums to remove the mystery surrounding the product. Provide simple ways for customers to research problems and find solutions on their own terms.

3. **Shape your response to fit their response**

   Some customers want to vent frustration, some want to tackle the problem, some want to avoid the problem. Be ready with a response to fit their response. Listen sympathetically to frustration. Provide resources to customers wanting to tackle the problem. Be ready to take over and handle everything for customers wanting to avoid the problem.

4. **Listen to the voice of the customer**

   Customers want the product to work well. Listen to what they have to say and make adjustments before one helpful voice turns into a large angry chorus.

Entrepreneurs can help themselves by responding to product imperfections using the **ABCs** of crisis management: **acknowledge**, **become** part of the solution, and **change** or continue to communicate about change.

It is a simple process. When a problem surfaces, acknowledge the problem with gratitude. For example, smile and say something like, "Thank you for bringing this to our attention. We want to continue to improve our product and this is something we haven't addressed yet." Then continue by becoming part of the solution, saying, "We meet every week to address product improvements; can we get back with you about our ideas?" Finally, follow up with a change and let the customer-turned-consultant know the outcome. Admittedly, having someone criticize your product feels a lot like listening to someone criticize your favorite child. Following the ABC process makes it easier for you and the customer. With the process, you don't have to get defensive and customers don't have to get frustrated.

What to Do to Guarantee Failure

Rather than trying to think of all the things that guarantee a perfect product, let's turn the problem on its head by thinking of all the things that guarantee failure. Entrepreneur and marketing consultant Roger Cauvin gets us started in the right direction by pointing out five sure ways to develop a losing product.

1. **Focus on how instead of what**
   Frustrate and restrict your design team by specifying how to meet a set of requirements rather than fully explaining what the requirements need to be.

2. **Don't ask customers why**
   Chase your tail reacting to customer demands by never asking why something is important. Be an expert at treating symptoms rather than getting to core issues.

3. **Write up all product requirements upfront and freeze them**
   Blissfully ignore unanticipated problems or emerging customer needs. Think everything through on your own and dodge designer-user iterations.

4. **Gloss over nonfunctional requirements**
   Forget about exploring and refining requirements like ease of use, sense of style, fit, and finish. After all, the only thing that matters is function.

5. **Specify, don't design the user interface**
   Decide what you want for a user interface with the product and go with it. Everyone should view the product the same way that you do. Turn a blind eye to usability issues that early-to-adopt customers may have.

After looking at this list, all we can say is "mea culpa." Summing up the advice, entrepreneurs guarantee failure when they tell and don't listen—when they design exclusively in their own world and don't find ways to connect with the world of customers.

Unleash the Power of Prototyping

The statistics prove it: finding product gold is a numbers game, and entrepreneurs need to sort through concepts quickly to identify those with the greatest potential, i.e., the WOW! Factor. We need a tool for sorting. We recommend prototyping. It is an effective way to step through a lot of ideas with just a bit more formality than using simple verbal descriptions.

Prototypes can be constructed at three different levels of goodness or fidelity; low-fidelity, which is nothing more than a simple paper prototype; medium-fidelity, which is a tangible mockup; and high-fidelity, which is a working prototype suitable for field testing. Of the three levels, we believe a low-fidelity paper prototype is the way to go for entrepreneurs. Jared Spool and Carolyn Snyder, two experts in the paper prototyping of computer software, give us some basic steps that we can adapt for general use. To learn about a design, just draw all the components of a design on paper and put it in front of potential users.

When putting a prototype in front of potential customers, focus on how successfully customers can use the product, not on how much customers like it. Getting defensive about customer feedback won't help startups launch winning products. In addition, Jared urges developers to sidestep using the computer for drawing up the prototype, even to design computer software, because he sees that it only slows down the process. Here are the basics. You may need to do some experimentation and continue to adapt some of the steps to your own personal style or product type.

1. **Perfect the customer profile**
   Nail down the profile of the most important customer group that will use the product.

2. **Get a grasp on the tasks**
   Gain a solid understanding of how customers will be using the product before constructing the prototype.

3. **Identify the greatest risks**
   There never is time to test every aspect of a product. Focus on testing the riskiest aspects and components.

4. **Make drawings**
   Using separate pieces of paper, sketch out the overall product as well as the product parts that present the greatest risks. Draw a picture for each step in using the product. Drawings definitely don't need to be neat or professional.

5. **Talk through the process**
   Bring in potential customers. Have them walk through the drawings and describe what they are thinking all along the way.

We are not asking for opinions here; we want a step-by-step narrative of what goes through the user's mind.

6. **Revise, revise, revise**
   After observing several users, go back and revise the design and the drawings. Then bring in more people. Ask several "why" questions when you get surprised by user comments.

7. **Regroup and rethink**
   Now is the time to address unanticipated issues and observations. Does the product still have the WOW! Factor? Make a "go" or "no go" decision and then move forward.

Entrepreneurs have too much ground to cover to indulge in expensive mockups and field testing. This is definitely a situation in which some information is better than no information, but for which paralysis by analysis can quickly settle in. Entrepreneurs must avoid the temptation to analyze a problem to the point where all forward motion stops. If a product has a strong WOW! Factor, do a little polishing, then get it out there in the marketplace. Concentrate your efforts where the WOW! Factor is high.

Audit the Startup

Doing an audit of a startup business can be as time-consuming as going through a long series of checklists, questionnaires, and interviews or as easy as getting reliable answers to a few basic questions. While we often prefer the easy approach, sometimes using the more thorough approach is the only way to get reliable answers.

Accurate measurement is a combination of two elements, validity and reliability. Validity asks the question, "Are we measuring the right things?" Reliability asks the question, "If we interviewed many experts, would we get the same answers over and over again?" The SuperLaws and Best Practices provide us with validity, as they are derived from the experiences of successful entrepreneurs. Reliability is another issue. Entrepreneurs love their businesses to the point of sometimes losing

BOOM
┌─THOUGHT 7.2─┐
An objective *audit of your startup is a must. Aligning a new business with Best Practices can save it from never getting off the ground or suffering a slow death.*

objectivity. As they say, "love is blind." Consequently, we provide ideas for checklists, questionnaires, and interviews to help entrepreneurs see beyond blind love and devotion and find substantive ways to increase their level of success with the new business.

Checklists

Sharpen the Angle. The five components of this SuperLaw are (1) Need to Believe, (2) Reason to Believe, (3) Blows Away Expectations, (4) Quantifiable Support, and (5) Unique Product Claim. When evaluating a checklist of these items, keep in mind that a check for *unique product claim* is earned by delivering strong in creating a new product category. That is, when reviewing a startup, we must ask ourselves whether it has truly carved out a little spot of blue in the Red Ocean most businesses and products swim in.

Even the 1970s fad, Rock Bottom Productions' Pet Rock, earned its uniqueness by creating a new category of pet. The Pet Rock alleviated the pain of wanting a pet, but not wanting to care for and clean up after a pet. It was unique and even made a personal statement of sorts. Its smooth, round, rock-solid construction sure made it look like a fun, maintenance-free pet, and owners could even add a set of glue-on eyes. Also, the Pet Rock blew away expectations of what one would think a rock could do. It was sold in a custom cardboard pet carrier, lying comfortably on its straw-like packing material, and had its own training manual with commands you could teach your new pet, such as sit, stay, roll over (with a little help), and attack. But as the saying goes, "big problem, big opportunity"—the Pet Rock did not address a big problem, and consequently its sales faded away in little more than six months.

Ride Horses. Are you trying to develop the idea, bring on investors, and sell to customers all by yourself, or do you have some powerful help? The checklist for *riding horses* includes: the business (1) has identified and engaged larger, better-funded benefactors that will succeed when the new business succeeds, (2) has distributed a "beta" version of the product from which it is compiling a list of future customers and getting feedback on improvements for the current design, (3) is making sales to small customers and currently engaged with a long-sales-cycle "elephant" customer, (4) has made a sale to an anchor customer or entered into talks with one or more anchor customers, (5) is elevating its partners, customers, and employees to hero status, (6) is finding ways for its "brand champions" to help promote and sell the business and its products, and (7) is creating a we-oriented culture and hiring employees that bring positive mojo as well as great skills to the business.

Play Big. Is your business a poser or are you engaged in legitimate activities that will help you play big? That is, is the business (1) developing relationships with and entering into a sales cycle with several large customers and investors rather than limiting itself to only one, (2) tapping into the benefits of being an underdog, such as brashness and daring to do things in their own way, (3) using a catchphrase that expresses the key benefit of the business with energy and memorability, (4) effectively using touch points to build strong relationships with customers and investors, and (5) building a spider web of advisors and learning from their experience?

Do an Event. Is your business relying on advertising such as flyers, magazine ads, billboards, and radio ads, or are you investing in events? Specifically, are you (1) creating experiential events that provide ways for customers to take the "consumption experience" into their homes, (2) throwing a "Love Fest" that brings together fully engaged "brand champions" with potential buyers, and (3) developing compelling product demonstrations that will grab the attention of potential buyers and generate Internet buzz?

Reap the Rewards. Now that you have the perfect angle, are you making all the money you deserve to? The checklist for reaping the rewards of your great idea and efforts includes: is the business (1) "asking for the sale" with confidence and directness every time they meet with a potential buyer or investor, (2) lowering barriers for buyers by offering guarantees, warranties, low-cost trials, addictive samples, etc., (3) establishing a value price that captures "what the market will bear," but not generating profits so high as to attract larger, better-funded competitors, (4) selecting the right place and right time to sell in order to maximize price and unit sales, and (5) introducing new products and services to augment the original product to gain greater share-of-wallet from "brand champions"?

Customer Questionnaires

New products will struggle along and have a hard time surviving unless they stir up a lot of passion with customers. Questionnaires can provide valuable feedback to entrepreneurs about the strength of their product concepts. To get a sense of the passion, entrepreneurs can explore the loyalty of early adopters by asking closed-ended "rating scale" questions such as:

1. Compared to similar products, how satisified are you with the performance of this product?
2. How likely are you to continue purchasing this product in the future?
3. How enthusiastic are you about recommending this product to a friend or family member?

Also, questionnaires can help entrepreneurs better appreciate the value customers believe they get from their products. Try asking early adopters open-ended questions such as:

1. Please look at this list of products [include the new product] and list them in order from "most likely to purchase" to "least likely to purchase" in the future.
2. What problem does this product solve for you [referring to the new product]?
3. In what ways does it solve this problem better than other products on the list?
4. Of the things you mention, which is the most important to you?
5. What is it about this product that gives it this ability?
6. On a personal level, what does it mean to you to get this problem solved?

There is no need to talk to thousands or even hundreds of people to get a good reading on a new product. Asking the questions listed above with a few dozen early adopters will provide a treasure trove of useful information that will keep the product on track, help with marketing communications, and better inform current and potential investors.

Personal Interviews

Venture capital firms and other potential investors don't usually want to take the time to fill out questionnaires, even short ones, so we recommend asking a few questions in person, online, or over the phone. The interviews should cover at least two areas: the business team and the business model. Of course, if the potential investor wants to keep talking about other aspects of the new venture, all the better.

The Business Team. Ask about impressions regarding the depth of experience, enthusiasm, and teachability of the business team. Investors are looking for a mixture of mature "been there and done that" with youthful exuberance and determination. In many cases, investor dollars depend more on the quality of the team than on the initial quality of the business idea.

The Business Model. How much revenue will the business generate as it matures? Is it a $2 million business, a $10 million business, a $100 million business? The size of the opportunity will dictate the type of investor the entrepreneur should consider. Venture capital firms rarely take on projects unless the opportunity is $100 million or more. In addition to raw revenue generation, also gather impressions about potential profitability, scalability, and ability to hold off competitors, large and small.

Using the Startup Audit

A Category Is Born. Scuba diving off the coast of Brazil, Nate Alder, the founder of Klymit, learned about how noble gases, like argon, xenon, and krypton are used as insulators inside of dry suits to keep divers warm. Building on that idea, the former snowboard instructor quickly envisioned how the "dry suit" technology could be adapted to insulate winter gear. While insulated clothing is nothing new, using valve-controlled linings in clothing to regulate temperature is new. There is no bulk, no layering, just turn the dial up and down. If a skier is cold, add a little argon

BOOM
—THOUGHT 7.3—

Entrepreneurs have a hard time being objective when auditing their own startup. Seek feedback from potential customers and outside experts to get a fair assessment of a business.

gas to the jacket lining. If a skier is hot, open the valve and release some argon to cool down.

One might think that Nate was only one prototype jacket away from hitting the entrepreneurial jackpot, but much was done to push the idea toward success. Nate's Director of Business Development felt there were ways to improve their chances for success and looked to the startup audit for ideas.

Working the Angles. Noble gas insulation for winter wear is a *unique product claim* backed up by *quantifiable support* such as: (1) several times more efficient at insulating than the current leading fabrics, (2) completely non-toxic, non-reactive, and non-flammable, and (3) heat-welded seams that eliminate leaks in the insulation. Also, it is a cold-weather clothing product that can *blow away expectations,* particularly for skiers and other outdoor sportsmen, because it is warmer, thinner, and lighter than anything else they have ever worn and can adjust to match their personal temperature. On the other hand, the audit revealed that people love the idea when they hear about it initially, but they later express concerns about the technology because it is hard for them to comprehend how the product works and whether the product can actually be relied upon in extreme conditions.

The team didn't do a good job of communicating a strong *reason to believe*, and this invited skepticism. To counter the weakness, the business created a series of compelling demonstration videos to tell their story to consumers, manufacturers, and investors using vivid pictures and industry experts. They also created specific product- and technology-centered videos that explain in simple terms why the technology can be relied upon, and how it works. All of these videos were integrated into a website that is designed to educate the consumer about the benefits of the technology and interest them in purchasing products.

Round Up the Horses. From the outset, Nate understood how to network and recruit horses. His biggest successes have been with a local mayor that wants to make his city the skiing mecca of the US, who has introduced Nate to a number of leading outdoor companies and investors. One of those companies is now a primary development partner, and several of those investors helped fund the business. Nate also was introduced to an industry "graybeard," an individual with decades of experience in the outdoor markets, who began assisting the company as a consultant. This connection alone has opened a number of closed doors.

The team was convinced early on that they couldn't bring insulation products to market on their own. They decided to identify large, well-funded "benefactor" companies that would benefit from adopting the new approach to insulation and license the technology. Within a year, the company secured "letters of intent" from three top outdoor brands that expressed great interest in adopting the patented technology for use in jackets, boots, snow pants, sleeping bags, and other products. Nate is hoping to land an *anchor customer* to sustain his young business among these first three companies, while knocking off some *rabbit customers* along the way.

Klymit prospects for *beta goldmines* with many companies, in which the companies purchase parts for prototypes and go through a beta testing period. Because the technology is so new and intersting, they want the chance to try it out, and Klymit has found it to be a great chance for expanding their potential customer list. Additionally, the mangement team has been very creative in applying the *Love Group* and *positive mojo* best practices. They used a logo design contest at a local college campus to create buzz and get a logo for cheap. They have leveraged business plan competition events to gain international acclaim and new brand champions, which has led to features in publications like *Fortune Small Business, Inc. Magazine*, CNN.com, and others. They found an intellectual property law firm that got excited about the technology, and the firm, in turn, has recently highlighted the business in local advertising, free of charge. They demonstrate the technology to every friendly face they meet and have opened their doors to individuals who have exciting ideas for new ways to use the technology and want to get involved.

BOOM
—THOUGHT 7.4—
Entrepreneurs must hit each SuperLaw, but don't need to apply every Best Practice. Each SuperLaw contains several Best Practices. Only apply those most relevant to your business.

Playing Big. Nate describes his product as the "Holy Grail of Insulation," a brash statement from a company that is determined to play big. Although just a startup with only two full-time employees, the business has engaged in activities that show they aren't going to let any opportunity pass them by.

It helps that Nate has created an advisory board and investor network that can be called upon for support and experience when needed; however, the day-to-day battle between David and Goliath is being led by the business's two full-time employees. After realizing that an early, smaller customer was interested enough in the technology to sign a letter of intent, the company began targeting larger, more established companies to see if they could generate interest. Result: the business has attracted attention from C-level executives at several of the world's largest multinational sports apparel companies, and executed in-person meetings with each of these companies, several of which agreed to test the technology. This has led the startup to believe that no customer is untouchable, and that limiting yourself to one partner will not allow you to realize your full potential.

Some company executives have been surprised to meet the faces behind the product, and to see that those faces are sometimes 30 years younger than their own. However, they have also come to recognize the excitement, determination, and daring of a team of young entrepreneurs who are not discouraged by the size of a potential customer. It may turn out that the startup finds that it is in its best interest to go with a number of smaller, more agile customers; but regardless of the final decision, it is certain that the attention given to the new technology by these large, well-established brands has increased Klymit's value in the eyes of its other smaller customers, which could end up paying off in a big way.

The Main Event. The Klymit team aggressively seeks out events to highlight their technology. They have participated in more than eight regional and national business plan competitions as well in numerous speed-venturing events in which they have "speed pitched" many dozens of investors, ranging from private investors and angels to venture capital firms and private equity financers.

The team is now considering ways to bring together "brand champions," beta testers, and other potential buyers into a "kontrol the elements" *Love Fest* with industry "graybeard" keynote speakers to build momentum for the company and shorten the sales cycle by creating a forum for manufacturers to share positive experiences they've had with the new technology. The team also is working on sample garments that will serve as centerpieces in a series of hands-on product demonstrations that will add drama and palpability to trade show and manufacturer demonstrations.

Positioned for Profit. Klymit's business model is focused on licensing technology and consequently operates outside the domain of guarantees, warranties, and addictive samples. Nevertheless, the management team has lowered barriers to adoption by offering *beta customers* access to low-cost trials. They have also been careful to propose licensing agreements that manufacturers in their key vertical markets find reasonable and affordable.

Klymit is also exploring a full range of applications in the ski industry in order to gain the greatest possible share-of-wallet from their "brand champions." Also, it is impossible to overemphasize the postive impact of participating in speed-venturing events. After speed-pitching for the 30th or 40th time, the team has learned how to present their ideas using easy-to-understand diagrams and explanations, which in turn makes it easy for the team to have confidence and "ask for the sale" every time they meet with a potential buyer, investor, or anyone else that can move them down the road to entrepreneurial success.

BOOM
THOUGHT 7.5

Startup audits must be focused on "how to" recommendations. Pointing out weaknesses without pointing the new business to a solution is pointless!

Review Questions

Define with Five

Define the following vocabulary words using five words or less.

1. WOW! Factor

_____

2. Prototyping

_____

3. Paralysis by Analysis

_____

4. Validity

_____

5. Reliability

_____

Question the Answer

Answer each phrase below in the form of a question.

1. On average, has about a one-in-10 chance for success.

_____

2. Beyond a strong WOW! Factor, these go a long way for startups in creating a forgiving attitude among customers.

_____

3. Tell, don't list, design products, and do not connect with customers.

---

4. If you are developing the idea, bringing in investors, and selling to customers all on your own, then you are not doing this.

---

5. Being more than a poser by engaging in legitimate image-building activities that enhance business credibility.

Smarter than an Entrepreneur

Name the product or venture that reinforces or violates a Boom Start best practice.

1. This company was born when the founder discovered some Blue Ocean while scuba diving off the coast of Brazil.

---

2. For this product, the WOW! Factor emerges from a fog of liquid nitrogen.

---

3. These blunt objects have a sharp angle.

---

4. This product made people tilt their heads slightly to the left and say, "WOW!"

---

5. Brashly describe their products as the "Holy Grail of Insulation."

SuperLaws in Action

The Startup Audit is a quick way to assess a business and find ways to improve its competitiveness. The key with the audit is to be honest and objective. Just think of it as tough love.

Activity: Find a small or startup business in the local community to study. Go through each of the SuperLaws and make at least one suggestion per law on how the business can improve their competitiveness and profitability.

Name of the business, location, and a brief description:

Suggestions on how to *Improve the Angle*:

Suggestions on how to *Ride Stronger Horses*:

Suggestions on how to *Start Playing Bigger*:

Suggestions on *Doing an Engaging Event*:

Suggestions on how to *Begin Reaping More Profits*:

Index